VIRALITY OF EVIL

VIRALITY OF EVIL

Philosophy in the Time of a Pandemic

Edited by
DIVYA DWIVEDI

ROWMAN & LITTLEFIELD
Lanham • Boulder • New York • London

Published by Rowman & Littlefield
An imprint of The Rowman & Littlefield Publishing Group, Inc.
4501 Forbes Boulevard, Suite 200, Lanham, Maryland 20706
www.rowman.com

86-90 Paul Street, London EC2A 4NE

British Library Cataloguing in Publication Information Available

Library of Congress Cataloging-in-Publication Data

Names: Dwivedi, Divya, editor.
Title: Virality of evil : philosophy in the time of a pandemic / edited by Divya Dwivedi.
Description: Lanham, Maryland : Rowman & Littlefield, [2021] | Includes bibliographical references and index.
Identifiers: LCCN 2021043913 (print) | LCCN 2021043914 (ebook) | ISBN 9781538164709 (cloth) | ISBN 9781538164723 (epub)
Subjects: LCSH: Good and evil. | COVID-19 (Disease) | Philosophy.
Classification: LCC BJ1405 .V57 2021 (print) | LCC BJ1405 (ebook) | DDC 170—dc23
LC record available at https://lccn.loc.gov/2021043913
LC ebook record available at https://lccn.loc.gov/2021043914

CONTENTS

INTRODUCTION

Divya Dwivedi

The provenance of this book of essays was in a symposium held virtually in June 2020, the late days of the first wave of COVID-19 pandemic in many parts of the world. It was to be a large conference on 'Confronting Evil' planned by several of us together with UNESCO and the Collège de France, which would have been the culmination of a number of preparatory colloquia and smaller conferences that took place since 2017. This project was collectively conceived in the urgency with which we were peering at the silhouette of this epoch in which suffering and deprivation have become so acute and intransigent that to speak of solutions and the good life seems contemptuous and even harmful, and a dull nihilism seems to be the only acceptable analytic today. The thinking of action, values and responsibility has given way to the thinking of impersonal, inevitable processes, catastrophes, collapses, apocalypse. It is that which appears to us, drives us, as one of the tasks of philosophy today: to re-examine the conceptions of desired futures and of responsibility under the heading of 'evil', the term which, through its opposition to 'good' – in a succession of theological, metaphysical and political conceptions of it – had served to open new epochs, to discover new futures, in the *criticalisation* of old ones. As Robert Bernasconi said in one of the conferences in 2019, *evil is perhaps the only question for philosophy today.*

Like many other projects, the conference had to be indefinitely postponed due to the viral pandemic. And yet, unlike many of them it was as if, by the very topic that was agitating and animating us, our plans were a recognition, anticipation and diagnosis, of a state or a condition (and not at all an event) that had already taken hold and was awaiting or wanting nothing other than its full articulation in all components of the world so that it could no longer be denied by those who obstinately still believed in the schema of 'norms and exceptions'.[1] The pandemic has achieved this articulation. It is, therefore, not the viral disease that is evil. Rather, a condition for which we have as yet no other designation than evil (this old, ambiguous name, as it must have also appeared to Hannah Arendt when she began to write on the European extermination of Jews in the last century) has become viral, in the etymological sense of poison and the media-theoretic sense of virality as an uncontrollable spread. And so in the place and time of the vacated plans, we decided to hold another, urgent, swift gathering like the witches of *Macbeth*, to speak of this state, speak to it, for it is our own – evil. If only under the hesitating title which yet confesses a terrifying suspicion: *Is it possible to speak of evil in the time of the pandemic?* This question itself is our responsibility, whose gravity was shown by Derrida when he said, 'The condition of possibility of this thing called responsibility is a certain experience and experiment of the possibility of the impossible'.[2]

As though we knew that the next time could be in thunder, lightning, rain or some other peril – and it did happen that my dear friend, Bernard Stiegler, who was co-organising the postponed conference, could not join the symposium due to ill health, and soon after, he left us forever – for we have as much to do as *Macbeth* with crimes foretold, cares abandoned, cries unheard, with deeds of men and women disguised in the voices of either nature or the supernatural, with ambitions that do not understand themselves.

We are still on the heath. And above too many, it is thundering.

'It' – the nameless, person-less, non-subjective 'it' of 'it rains', the 'it' that Heidegger held as the task of thinking. Quotidian grammar allows anything to be it. It is evil, it is the pandemic, it is above all a general plight bearing the imprint of the human hand but being at the same time beyond its grasp. It marks the place of misadventure, misfortune, misdirections, but also mischances, méconnaisance, misnomers.

Immediately, 'it' is the pandemic. 'It' is also a previously forming condition of which the pandemic is only a symptom and a metonymy. COVID-19 is as much a concrete and particular calamity as it is a misnomer. The present worldwide suffering is only partly a medical affliction due to the viral disease, rather it is a situation of economic, psychological, political hardship extended over a long period now without an end in sight. It is a sharing and distribution of wretchedness and insecurities related to occupation, health care, displacement, environmental degradation and the rise of populism as well as of far-right and far-left political groups.[3] It is the entanglement of biological and civilisational seizure or a 'general equivalence' as Jean-Luc

Nancy proposed in the immediate context of the Fukushima nuclear disaster, and which he describes in his chapter in this volume as 'a doubt [. . .] What if there was a structural evil in that which today produces and conditions the human species, including – or, in fact, first – where they appear comfortable and conquering'?[4] The pandemic as a devastating medical state, but further as an uncontrollable magnification and multiplication of misery, loss and incapacities, was possible because of a malaise greater than viral infections. This magnitude is only one reason to speak of evil.

The other is that the origins and trajectories of this malaise are human actions embarked upon through rationalisations, decisions, deeds of humans and their institutions. And hence the concept of evil bequeathed by Immanuel Kant as the ownmost possibility of human freedom rather than a theological enigma of a godhead. The banalisation, as Hannah Arendt put it, of evil referred to the condition where human beings turned themselves into obedient servants of a thinking that happened 'elsewhere' – leaders, parties. Today, this 'elsewhere' is the internet forums, social media and conspiracy theories.

Institutions which were designed, and promised, to harbour the freedom and possibility of thinking – democracy, journalism, judiciary, university, art and literature – have now become the indefinite exile of thinking, and we no longer have the conditions for deliberation or critique, which therefore can no longer be the means for their own recovery. All components that make up our worldwide, mutually comprehending existence – and which divide men into colours, collars, castes – are straining, faltering. The hands of some are bloodier than most, but the world is haemorrhaging too rapidly. There are no Macbeths or even Eichmanns today, but technology corporations and financial corporations who proclaim to think for the world. This is evil become viral, decimating the very world in which it earlier corrupted individuals or despoiled regions (which are nothing but the confinement of man whose world is already a ruin).

But the unnameable and therefore infinite demand of life does not lift. Death is only a more or less long run, running ahead to the past as Heidegger said, and we stretch the interval not to postpone or avoid death but to live just long enough to invent the senses and directions of life, which we also, therefore, suffer. Whence our terror at no longer being able to find an interval, to *do the interval*; which is the terror at what I have elsewhere called the *great isolation*: that this worldwide confinement has functionally isolated of the whole world into a single function, that of coping with the pandemic, but that this great isolation cannot endure indefinitely (as it now appears to be doing), rather it must be a transitory isolation.[5]

Symposia and books are luxuries, according to a certain measure. But they are nevertheless, and nothing other than, intervals which are necessary for philosophy as that which creates the conditions to imagine and realise another world. Because nothing less than an inventive relation to the present will do, and everything through which we as a world could invent sense is depleted, turned destructive. There are no special units for the critical care of a world.

Not the least sign of this is the poverty of the very concepts with which to speak of the pandemic: 'war', 'crisis', 'state of exception'. We must heed with utmost care what Shaj Mohan has called to our attention:

> Crisis is managed through the additions and subtractions of components on the one hand and through the prescription of new regularities on the other. In a way this is how we have been trying to handle the world in recent years; we fire a few teachers in the universities and raise money from entrepreneurial programs; we bring austerity measures and lower taxes for the rich; we drop bombs with drones and maintain kill lists; reduce a few motor cars in the cities while burning more coal for electricity. In this sense we have been in crisis for a long time now. We have been even calling it a permanent crisis. How come we never found the adequate exchanges, transplants, and new regularities to find a way towards a recovery process? It is because we are not in crisis.

Crisis is an inadequate designation for where we are today.[6]

The first need, therefore, is to find ways to speak of the evil, which is our own condition, and to find the occasions to think together and speak to each other. It is an evil in the time of the *pan*-demic that much of the theoretical reflection on it takes the first world's experience of COVID-19 and the confinement as the central reality, while the rest of the world is confined to numbers and graphs. Leaving aside the puzzles about the will to will, and the prayers to for grace to unify divided wills, we need those transitive acts of invention that can regain for us an interval. Faced with systemic evil they must be acts of collective thinking.

Evil is difficult to figure, it demands *muthos* – narrative, literature, cinema, triptychs, all of which are swallowed in the waves of destitution – but today it demands that we begin to see and speak of the world *as world*, the whole world, all of us, everyone, discarding the myths of local destinies that led us to identify ourselves with maps and orientations such as 'Occident', 'Orient', 'North and South'. In other words as the beings that I would call 'indestinate'.[7] Beyond even this, evil demands philosophy because we do not have the concepts yet to comprehend the evil that preceded, ushered, and now endures through, the pandemic. The very words with which to bring the present and the future to freedom, to collective and democratic imagination, action, invention, are not yet there. It is only in this, and in its *propos*, that we can create those words so that the world, which is now in stasis, can be brought to *anastasis*: a new relation to both philosophy and politics, and a new comprehension of the criticalised arrangements of our time so that new arrangements can take birth.

NOTES

1. Dwivedi and Mohan, 'Community of the Forsaken', 31.
2. Derrida, *The Other Heading*, 41.
3. See the discussions in the volume *Coronavirus and Psychoanalysis and Philosophy.*
4. See Nancy, *After Fukushima.*
5. Dwivedi, 'Through the Great Isolation', 17.
6. Mohan, 'But there is Nothing Outside of Philosophy'.
7. Dwivedi, 'A Flight Indestinate', 108.

BIBLIOGRAPHY

Derrida, Jacques. *The Other Heading: Reflections on Today's Europe.* Translated by Pascal-Anne Brault and Michael B. Naas. Bloomington: Indian University Press, 1992.

Dwivedi, Divya. 'A Flight Indestinate'. In *Coronavirus and Psychoanalysis and Philosophy*, edited by Fernando Castrillón and Thomas Marchevsky, 105–109. London: Routledge, 2021.

Dwivedi, Divya. 'Through the Great Isolation: Sans-Colonial'. *Philosophy World Democracy* 1, no. 1 (November 2021): 13–21. https://www.philosophy-world-democracy.org/through-the-great-isolation

Dwivedi, Divya and Shaj Mohan. 'Community of the Forsaken'. In *Coronavirus and Psychoanalysis and Philosophy*, edited by Fernando Castrillón and Thomas Marchevsky, 31–34. London: Routledge, 2021.

Mohan, Shaj and Rachel Adams. 'But there is Nothing Outside of Philosophy: Interview with Shaj Mohan'. *Philosophy World Democracy* 2, no. 2 (February 2021). https://www.philosophy-world-democracy.org/but-there-is-nothing-outside.

Nancy, Jean-Luc. *After Fukushima: The Equivalence of Catastrophes.* Translated by Charlotte Mandell. Fordham University Press, 2015.

Part I

ACTS OF EVIL

1

UP AGAINST THE WALL

Jean-Luc Nancy

Translated by Sindhuja Veeraragavan

1

For decades, and in the same half-century, a difficult question has worked and worried the mind.[1] This question most often takes the Freudian name of 'death drive'. The title of Buyung-Chul Han's most recent book – *Capitalism and Death Drive (Kapitalismus und Todestrieb)* – can be cited as an example. The title stands out, not only because of its two associating notions derived from vastly differing fields but also by the fact that it does not surprise us. We immediately get the feeling that we know what it is all about. We are even able to think that there is a 'sense of déjà-vu' (without insinuating by that any depreciation of the book in *question, but on the other hand, suggesting that it talks about a subject that is becoming a nagging worry for everybody).*

The interest in death drive (about which one can furnish a long list of recent references) has been accompanied by an interest in a notion less clearly linked to any discipline, but touched upon nevertheless by Freud: cruelty. On the one hand, numerous socio-historic works deal with cruel conduct in regard to torture, camps, genocides or ethnocides of every sort, and on the other hand, a philosophical and psychoanalytical preoccupation around the subject of cruelty has manifested in many ways, in Derrida, Lacan, Clément Rosset, Bernard Baas and Mirjam Schaub, among others. There too, we have a feeling of already-knowing and at the same time, we do feel a certain surprise at a theoretical interest for what seems immediately to be crystallized in the ignominy and unbearableness of barbarism – a term often associated with cruelty – quite simply alien to civilization and, therefore, to the dignity of thought.

Yet, civilization has been cruel, and that is not the least lesson to be drawn from the history of colonialism as well as that of exterminations, to which Europe served as the starting point, and she continues to be even as she worries increasingly about that which she is obliged to call her own barbarism (as it is still necessary to use this term that originally described the vulgar and confused manner of speaking of people that the Greeks considered to be without culture).

It is to this worry to which the enduring work on the notions of death drive and cruelty testify. One must not be led astray by the disciplinary categories that would lead one to believe that these are questions pertaining to psychoanalysis and/or socio-economics and ethics. These categories, on the contrary, risk blurring the perception of a reality that can but be termed as philosophical, not to mention metaphysical.

If I am using the latter word, it is because Freud himself referred to it when he invented the term 'metapsychology'. In coining this, he indicated that the biggest concern of his work was not psychological, that he could even cast doubt upon the very representation of 'psychism' distinct from that of a social, economic, political and cultural reality. To metapsychology belongs the study of drives – the *Triebe* whose nature remains 'mythical' to Freud, which first of all means that they are neither simply physical nor simply psychic, that they play out where the separation of these notions dissolve and also where the line between the personal and the collective vanishes. In other words, at the very place of human existence.

Freud here is the author of *Civilisations and its Discontents*, where he questions modern violence and its rapport with drives that civilization is supposed to overcome. The point at which we are almost a century later can be summed up under another title which would be *The Ill-being of civilization.*

Ill-being because it is more than malaise (a term Freud employed euphemistically). It is a question of disarray, of a more or less vivid awareness of a real disease – not the one stemming from a single virus but an infection that, for some reasons, may be called autoimmune – a term used for pathologies that cause an organism to self-destruct. Ill-being of – rather than in – the civilization, for it is in the heart or the soul of the civilization that this is caused. This fact was observed, at the same time as Freud, by Heidegger and Wittgenstein. Along with them, in his way, Franz Fanon talks of the necessity of 'changing one sort of mankind for the other'.

Of course, this defect which is in a way organic is not perceived – at least not in the same way – according to regions and peoples, because a characteristic of this civilization is that it concentrates its powers and their beneficence (or its benefits, according to the lexicon that one would prefer) to a very restricted part of humanity. The other parts strive to gain access to the well-being demonstrated by societies and/or classes considered developed. However, what is new is that, in these very societies/classes, a doubt has begun to arise. What if there was a kind of structural evil in that which today produces and conditions the human species, including – or in fact, first – where they appear comfortable and always conquering?

It is possible that the doubt aroused in the developed societies passes on to those aspiring for development, and that, moreover, the desire of the poorest is not simply regulated by the reproductive model of the West. Wanting a decent life takes on a material and moral sense that differs according to cultures of origin. Perhaps, too, the ecological necessities that are becoming urgent may influence these desires in their nature, without diminishing their power. (The many diverse expressions of sexual desire – from courtly love to rape – may be taken as an example here.)

2

If truth be told, violence and cruelty in all their forms are not entirely new. The wars of ancient centuries, massacres, and tortures – to say nothing of extortion, exploitation, all forms of domination – have not been absent in a large part of human cultures. What, however, has been as new as industrial modernity, is the perception, or at least the suspicion of a deliberate, intentional evil of which men are capable. And this also means the possibility of an ontological wickedness.

In European philosophy, this suspicion appears clearly in Kant and Schopenhauer. Following them, it has been sharpened towards the Freudian death drive and the denial of alterity as Sartre, Levinas or Derrida have variously identified. In a certain manner, it has always been about this: a refusal, a reduction or an exclusion of the other.

The term 'denial' is undoubtedly the best-suited one to characterize what is less an opposition to the other and more a desire to not have to deal with one's alterity. And this desire addresses just as much the subject's own alterity as that of the other subjects. It is in this condition that one can understand how the very principle of bad will emerges.

Radical evil, according to Kant, is an evil which has no preceding reason and which strictly comes under freedom as well as contrary disposition. To be itself, freedom must be free to deny that of the other, even if that means corrupting itself irremediably. In a similar way, one may say that the desire of the living, which is to live still, is being itself only if it recognizes its mortal alterity. The latter is presented – one is even tempted to say proposed – as something that the desire of life wants to overcome, but as also something into which it has an urge to precipitate.

Now, if one can speak of a man of modern civilization as a 'one dimensional man', as Marcuse did, it is possible for as long as single dimension, first of all, denies its own alterity. That is, both its own mortality and the existence of the other as the condition for my own human existence.

For an exclusive uniqueness to be possible, there needs to be a civilization in which nothing is foreign to man, the producer and the benefactor of his own existence. This means that this existence itself is a product and a consumer good. Hence, humanity is divided between a minority which enjoys living and a majority which aspires to be able to live.

The most elementary motive behind this unilaterality is property. That is, the clear idea of belonging: 'this is mine' but which could also be 'this is ours' in case of a national property or some such other collectivity. Appropriation is at the heart of all domination – and vice versa. On the contrary, that which would not be unilateral is the consideration of an *être propre*, the proper being, of each individual and each community. This proper being would neither be determinable nor exclusive: it necessarily implies a rapport with others. The proper being implies inappropriation and transpropriation. Marx, purposely or not, thought in this direction – after those before him who understood that property is the evil. It undermines the proper being.

The proper being – the self – is not the product of an appropriation (which would have no first subject!). It is, on the contrary, an interminable process (otherwise than by death) of a continuous transpropriation through which a primary appropriating individual (a feeding baby) spreads through renewed expropriations (it loses the 'in and of itself' in affect, language, work, sex and the alterity which will always have preceded and which will always follow). Derrida spoke of 'exappropriation': the 'proper' being its authority.

It is on the basis of a general law of appropriation that inequality itself becomes a law and the expropriating minority inflicts on the expropriated majority the suffering of a loss of livelihood, but at the same time, it inflicts on itself the absurdity of a life which is only supported on condition that it dominate, if possible, until death. This we call 'transhumanism', ignoring that fact that we are bringing back Dante's word (*trasumanar*) which did not at all mean going beyond the human but a form of joyful ecstasy.

Self-production and unlimited domination: this is the unique dimension which defines itself more or less expressly as 'good' and which does not realize that it does not absolutely know where this gigantic automatism is headed – other than towards a destruction that increasingly threatens human, animal and plant diversities, that is, life itself.

3

For this, certain conditions were necessary. The first is found in the indefinite increase in technical power. After having been through the stage of energy production, it went through the stage of information production. It may, perhaps, go through the stage of life production too. Yet, an integral self-production of life would be a contradiction, if life itself is alterity, alteration and strangeness of itself. The technical indefinite is a bad infinite, a leak in the enumeration of numbers.

The second condition is the increase in human population, such that questions arise, not only of survival and decent life of a great number, but also, undoubtedly and especially, the questions of relations between groups or communities, such that their very coexistence leads everyone to question their co-presence or their appearance in the same planetary or even the same cosmic space, as technologically, we have extended very far into the cosmos. This, moreover, has changed status: it is no longer the colossal whole of a universal order, but a complex, multiple and pulsing, spatio-temporal expanse that shares our wandering.

The third condition narrowly depends on the first two. The general growth of technical rationality (which also means – it should not be forgotten – medical, cultural, judicial) comes with a trend of wiping out all forms of legitimation. When legitimacy is wholly pertaining to what we call reason – calculating, demonstrative and operative reason – it can ultimately only take us back to the absence of the primary or the last reason, which is its fundamental state of being. Neither science, nor law, nor argumentation is made to get back to the principles – any more than they are made to achieve ends.

Property is found in the principle of all valid legitimacies: but if there is no founding reason, then it is necessary to admit that property cannot be one such reason and that it is necessary to go further.

This is known and recognized by all rigorous thought but hitherto no result has been rigorously derived from this. We persist in speaking vaguely of politics or the economy as though we have principles and ends at our command. But all legitimacies are suspended, the most traditional ones as well as the most recent (I mean here the Marxist legitimacy, because although the word 'Communism' might still mean a desired legitimacy, it no longer has any doctrine to stand on).

To be sure, religious legitimacies still play non-negligible roles. But they are most often enrolled in the service of politico-economic dominations. At the same time, what we call democracy displays everywhere – when it is not openly violated – great difficulty to legitimize itself without falling back on nationalism or without losing its way in good intentions. And always and everywhere, finally and for starters, appropriation remains a principle instead of submitting itself to the incalculable sovereignty of the self.

(Sovereignty – Bataille was able to capture its nature of 'NOTHING', as he calls it. That is to say that a supreme power has nothing to establish itself. Which doesn't eliminate the need for a power of decision, nor the impossibility of reducing decision to a rational choice – but lays bare the absence of ultimate legitimation. In other words, each sovereignty lays itself open to another – like the state to the people, each of the two remains a 'NOTHING'.)

For us, sovereignty is supposedly founded in nature or in reason – or yet, it appears to be a tyrannical caprice. And in fact, it can take all these forms. But techno-economic power governs everything and legitimizes itself through power and not through sovereignty. 'Hell is paved with good intentions' as the old proverb goes. We are not far from making the earth hell. With the most remarkable productions of the mind – from Indian mathematics to global nanotechnologies – we have ended up stripping ourselves of purpose. Each step forward comes with two steps backwards. We can longer reassure ourselves by saying that evil destroys itself, because this feedback is also that of what we call 'progress'.

Progress, henceforth, is only possible if it progresses towards another species of man, to use Fanon's words. We are up against the wall.

Whether it be in Africa or Europe, in Asia or the Americas, humanity has already been up against the wall more than once. This was the case of the Mediterranean world before the Greeks and the Jews, before Jesus and Mohammed, before the Western adventure. Before what, before who we are, we the late comers, who came ill-timed? Ahead of what? Ahead of whom?

NOTE

1. My thanks to Divya Dwivedi who contributed suggestions to the last version of this text.

2

MODALS OF LOST RESPONSIBILITIES

Divya Dwivedi

It is now unavoidable to talk about evil as we are aware that the majority of the world is suffering. We are also aware that this suffering, of which the pandemic is only a calamitous augmentation, was and is preventable since it is not a destiny but a state whose persistent conditions have been secured by the regularities that compose our world: institutionalised inequalities between people and communities, systemic reproduction of deprivation of the goods and the degradation of the environments that sustain life.

We also recognise that, nevertheless, specific powers available to a few men and institutions – economic, judicial, legislative, technological – preclude the majority from collectively accessing the means to prevent this widespread and acute suffering. The existence of these regularities renders all thought of an ontological 'precariousness', of a historical destiny of Being, as well as of evil as a theological problem, to be a mockery of the suffering of the majority of people in the world. Rather, evil, in the sense bequeathed to us by Hannah Arendt, concerns the sphere of collective human actions and their consequences, that is, evil concerns social formations and politics.

We experience a difficulty in finding the words to describe to each other this situation since many words such as evil, bad, freedom, reason, fact, even politics, have become unavailable for having been functionally isolated by a rhetoric that makes them meaningless and even dangerous – the 'axis of evil' as a term deployed in order to bomb and gas a whole people; 'Freedom' as the name of a far-right party in Europe. Our situation is like the one we find in the poem 'Die Schleuse' (The sluice) by Paul Celan:

lost
I lost a word
that had remained with me
. . .
I lost a word that was looking for me
. . .
Through
the sluice I had to go,
to salvage the word into the saltflood back
and out and across:
Yizkor[1]

That is, the third word is the one that neither 'remains' nor 'looks for' the poet persona, but rather it is a word that itself needs salvaging through a difficult act, a struggle. Etymologically, loss comes from the Old English and Old high German *los* meaning ruin and dissolution. We receive the hint offered by Celan that to *come over* the most devastating experience is a struggle which has a poetic dimension where *poiesis* is not the invention of fictions or metaphors nor a self-referential play of language, but a new comprehending of the debris of the day that would lead into a new future. It is also an intimation, given the evil of Holocaust that was the context of the poem, that the most devastating experiences are the progeny of a whole arrangement in which sufferings are dispensed and words are withdrawn, and which arrives differently to every epoch. To imagine an exit from an epochal arrangement cannot be done on the basis of the values and ends that were meaningful within it, such is the extent of the devastation and loss that is systemically engendered. Rather, it requires that the epoch would have to be comprehended at the point of its exhaustion or criticalisation, where the debris is beheld as such – as another of Celan's late poems in *Eingedunkelt* asks, 'Fill the wasteland in the eye-sacks'[2] – having become the material awaiting new means and new ends. And this needs a new word or a renewed word and a new way of speaking it – parole, poiesis! – for which we must struggle.

Hence, the word at stake is not this or that privileged word, myth or revelation but, above all, language itself, that is, the community that words form with each other when something is communicated. Which is why the poet gives to everyone and no one the many words composed as a poem or *parole* in order to remind us that what one looks for – and has lost in the sense that one does not already have access to it – is 'a word'. Which is why Kant was already showing us in the form of 'the public use of reason' that we have the responsibility of exchanging words with each other about what concerns us all, indeed of discovering anew and together what might concern us all. Which is why man has been called the animal that can make promises, that can give its word, and can by means of promises, plans and actions, bind itself to ends of its own making, that is, a definite future which would go 'out and across', shared with others. Word and act have their jointure in this ability to respond to each other and to take responsibility.

Before the mysteries of the divided will as in Augustine, or of *Wille* and *Willkür* in Kant or of the *will to will* in Heidegger's Nietzsche, the word 'evil', once displaced to the level of banality by Arendt, belongs with the concern with freedom and human thinking and acting. At this level, another word, hardly a word but rather an auxiliary to words and to language, speaks in it – 'should have'. In the recent decades we had been looking for this word on the occasion when one cannot turn away from the thought that some X *should not have* happened. 'Evil' is the word for this regarding of the world through an eye-sack stuffed with devastation, that is, with the knowledge that some X *should have been* prevented.

The literature abounds which analyses the many things that should have been done to mitigate the arrival of an epidemic and to prevent it from becoming a pandemic, and then a prolonged one as it now is, and also the many things that should not have been done. All these analyses address themselves to the present arrangement of the components of our world which are not in the grasp of individuals but have been maintained by massive technological corporations, economic organisations and then nation-states which conduct their crony function by deploying the hoaxes of national, racialised and religious identities in some cases and of their postcolonial victimhood in others. These last have withdrawn from the function of the state which was to look after the people, and have instead perfected a murderous population politics of discrimination and legal as well as illegal persecution which they perpetrate on citizens and refugees with impunity. The experience of the pandemic, with its specificities according to local conditions in different parts of the world, has been a combination of new shocks to the system where it worked for the privileged sections of societies, and an intensification of the old suffering that was distributed according to pre-existing relations of inequality and deprivation. The viral disease reached all the regions of the world geopolitically identified as 'east', 'west', 'global north' or 'global south', but as during Hurricane Katrina, the collapse of economies and public health, as in the case of medicines and vaccination, has been and will continue to be worse for the poor than the rich, the blacks than the whites in the United States, the lower castes (which make up the majority of the poor, the labourers and the unemployed in India) than upper castes.

These pre-existing tendencies of the world's arrangement evidence the overwhelming and worldwide stability of the conditions of evil. It is a sad reflection on contemporary humanities and social sciences that the only recently experienced economic insecurity of previously affluent groups in Europe and North America has been elevated into a theoretical framework called *precarity* and even into an ontologically fundamental attribute of human life called *precariousness*, this elevation erases the trenchant miseries of the wretched of the earth and averting them from our eyes. The conceptual dyad of precarity/security is informed by the nostalgia for a non-precarious, that is, delectable stable past which is, in the words of Shaj Mohan, the *idyllic a priori* of a privileged few[3] and which the majority of the world can experience only vicariously. The scholars of precarity and precariousness ignored the fact that there is nothing precarious in the suffering inflicted on non-White people in the Americas through slavery, or on Dalits in India through the apartheid of the caste order. Rather, their oppressions and its descent-based inheritance in every new generation continues to be secured since centuries and the term precarious does not reflect their realities or those of many other similar populations in the world. Equally, to elevate economic precarity (with its attendant sufferings which are real and deplorable no matter how few undergo them) into an ontological attribute is to mask the stable differences and inequalities that actually exist between different sections of societies; it is also to mask the sustained ways in which the same agents (e.g., the U.S. government) have been acting in ways that have resulted in choreographing the devastation of other parts of the world (Iraq, Libya), which therefore have no COVID-care to speak of.

It is this particular pre-existing arrangement that has received the viral epidemic. It is many human and institutional acts of commission and omission that have granted the pandemic proportions, despite being in possession of the cumulative knowledge of the previous epidemics in our century, the wilfully underfunded scientific researches and the humanities and social sciences. That is why the viral variants and deadly symptoms may continue to evade an effectual understanding, but the fact that the pandemic would affect every component of the world as it does has not surprised us from the very beginning. The word 'evil' announces itself in the face of this contrived incapacity in our encounter with an epidemic. The expectability of the pandemic is and *should have been* the measure for thinking and transforming the worldwide arrangement. What seems urgent to reflect on is the responsibility that is imposed on us by its acknowledgment – *should have.*

This *should have been*, the whisper of responsibility, is the mode of recognition of mistakes as well as the mode of those apologies which are not a mere gesture but an admission of a regretted act, whether committed, omitted or witnessed, which simultaneously binds the speaker to the futures adumbrated by the admitted crime. We have already known that apologies without punishments and reconciliations without truths evade precisely this bond which demands actions, namely that we must act to not let it happen again. The bond, then, includes but exceeds the individual agent of the crime because it binds all the institutions that are implicated in the recognition of the crime and its future prevention, and therefore binds all of us who are implicated in these institutions and their constitution in whatever degree and capacity. The people of the world enacted this responsibility when they demonstrated in different countries against the killing of George Floyd by the police in the United States. The suffering brought down upon so many leading to and in this pandemic is of immense magnitude and the word we must insist on is the one that announces the collective resolve that would never let it happen again. It is the resolve and promise to each other on each other's behalf which speaks in the *should have been*.

Grammarians call the modal verbs *could have* and *should have* 'modals of lost opportunities', but this name focuses only on the attitude towards the individual past opportunity named in a locution. It misses the attitude evinced in the *should have* which is at once towards the past and future, and further, is of the nature of a word given to each other, an apology, a promise, a resolve. Let us call it more accurately *the modal of lost responsibilities*. Other verb forms related to this giving of a word together form the *modals of lost responsibilities*.

A misplaced humility cultivated by diverse nihilisms had been preventing us from admitting this thought of the modals of lost responsibility that murmurs through the word 'evil', as though one were claiming too much power in claiming a lost responsibility. There is a tendency to think that this pandemic announces the collapse of the 'modern' world which is said to have been built on a confidence in human powers to master nature leading to an inexorable and essentially colonialist process ever since the fifteenth or sixteenth century when 'modernity' displaced the old world.[4] Here too, the *idyllic a prior* reveals itself at work in the enchantment with a nostalgia for the old world and an active forgetting of its horrors. This tendency in thought posits a *destiny* for the world, whether of *progress* or *decline*, which corresponds to a 'proper' or authentic state for man, and unfolds as a single, essential history of the human sojourn on the planet. This is not the occasion to examine the varieties of such *destinal* auguries – of M. K. Gandhi, of the Freud in *Das Unbehagen in der Kultur*, Adorno and Horkheimer, Heidegger in the *Black Notebooks*, but we should heed Jean-Luc Nancy's warning against its dangerous consequences in Heidegger's thinking. For, it is to Heidegger's destinal thinking of 'the history of Being' that Nancy also traces Heidegger's banal anti-Semitism which was of a piece with all the clichés of his time):

> This amounts to confirming that nothing essential has happened in the destiny of the West – nothing except the aggravation of metaphysics and its technical and democratic becoming. Put another way, anti-Semitism is necessary to avoid speaking of anything at all as another *Geschehen* that would have happened or that would have been outlined here or there in the history of Europe.[5]

The banal and the destinal will often be found in macabre companionship as a false conception of our sojourn in the world that nevertheless has real effects and real victims. A thinking of one history supposes that the world is the stable matter that receives a form that will sustain. This is also the logic of a thinking that ontologises a feature of a particular social formation; in other words, one particular componential law (i.e., the law that specifies one of the regularities that comprise the world, say the present precarity of the Baby boomers generation) is privileged as the comprehending law of the entire arrangement of the world at a given time.

This is, perhaps, the most dangerous *méconnaisance* of all, since it simultaneously averts our attention from both the different sufferings in other parts of the world *and* from the deeper level at which these different components are reciprocally comprehended in a stable way so as to constitute an epoch, and yet in a perishable way such that they await their transformations which may open new epochs free of these oppressions. For instance, today's worldwide arrangement is controlled, without having uniform effects everywhere, by new agents – technology corporations and international economic organisations – and not by colonial formations of the last two centuries. We will not be able to address today's word-wide sufferings, including the pandemic, if we only address some particular components of the world while ignoring their comprehending law or identifying it with only one of the components. And in affixing destinies, of which many models are being offered today – decoloniality, biopolitics, Anthropocene – we will also be averted from the transformative possibilities, and hence freedom, which await their discovery in every shift from one comprehending law to another.

This shift bespeaks the *indestinacy* of the world. The world itself has no destiny, for it is forsaken by transcendent ends. This is the sense of loss that Rilke expressed:

Du im Voraus
verlorne Geliebte,
You from the outset
lost beloved,[6]

The world is the very place where worlds come and go. It is not the stable matter receiving moulds oriented by utopias or innate evil tendencies of man (or Western man), but neither is it a wholly un-stabilisable, free and precarious something that escapes human efforts and dooms them from the start. Rather the world manifests its mouldability and comports this indestinate passage by being at every moment an arrangement of regularities that are themselves the matter for new regularities comprehended in a new law. *Indestinacy* refers to what is lost from the start, and which thus permits freedom – the indestinate, therefore, which is us, is given to the possibilities of freedom to mould, freedom to unmould and freedom to be surprised. But these possibilities *arrive* and are *lost* in the present arrangements of regularities. The freedom to generate and share new possibilities is inseparable from our sense of the material ways in which regularities that arrange our lives are made and unmade. This sense, that we can imagine ways of unmaking the present arrangement of regularities, obliges us to fight for them. *Politics* is nothing other than this fight in the world in the present, for the sake of the worlds awaiting us.

Hence, politics is a fight born of the responsibility of us all for the whole world. Democracy is the other name for this responsibility which we share with each other. And in our epoch where all flows and all problems are connecting the whole world, responsibility as well as democracy cannot be regionalised. Instead, we are now concerned with the democracy of the world so that the people of the world who are all affected by the globally impacting decisions of technocratic corporations but who have never been consulted in these decisions can finally participate in the arranging of their lives.

The acknowledgement of evil as obliging our collective thought and action is what speaks in the modal of lost responsibilities, the thought of human responsibility, political responsibility and collective responsibility. Beyond guilt and recompense it obliges us to imagine and realise new regularities that would prevent known evil from repeating, and this can only be done by exchanging words and promises with each other.

Let us pay careful attention to what language says in the modal form and the past tense of the '*should have been*'. Modals in general, such as *should, could, will, must, have to,* have to do with permission, obligation, compulsion, desire, readiness and will be associated with action. They are often considered not to be verbs at all but auxiliaries which refer to the degree of modifications of an action. Languages have other ways of evincing this auxiliary function, for instance saying *have to* instead *must*: Celan's 'through/ the sluice I *had to* go'. Languages allow us to express these modifications, to begin with, because they are essential participants in our understanding that things, people and their relations are susceptible to and even desirous of modifications: if Y is a mode of X then X is susceptible to more modifications than Y, Y', Y'' and so on; X can become A, and then A itself could be susceptible to other modifications. The simple formula *Y is a mode of X* does not allow us to see that modifications require conditions and pose the question of the modification of the very conditions so that we *shall* exit from the present regularities into new ones by modifying the functional isolations of things under newly imagined ends. It is how we have freedom, that is, varying degrees of modifiability of and distance from the past so that we can arrive at a new stance that is capable of seeing in the past other possibilities than were realised, that is, of imagining and legislating new regularities. This freedom is polynomia, the power in all things to become home to more than one regularity. But further, an obligation attaches itself to this freedom through the shall/shoulds, which etymologically traces to the speculative root *skel meaning *owe* or *obligation.*

The very past tense of the modal *should have* evinces this freedom as the recognition of that interval between the past and the present which is capable of polynomial games from the vantage of desired and imaginable futures. In this it is distinguished from the present tense of the auxiliaries *should* and *must.* The present tensed expressions of *must* enunciate an authoritative force bestowed on a particular action or its prohibition, while *should*, which expresses a weaker sense of obligation than *must*, enunciates an exhortation guided by the criteria for criticism which one possesses in accordance with a critique of present conditions, that is, an understanding of a system of limits. This is related to the way *should* also expresses likelihood, possibility and probability. But in the face of evil which is systemic and which therefore implicates the very conditions that obtain, in other words which *criticalises* the conditions and thus makes critique useless, a very different enunciation is needed which beholds the debris of criteria and critique and admits a loss that is more than the absence of a particular object for it is the loss of our powers of response in relation to that object. The temporal reference of *should have*, *should not have* and *should have been*, expresses this sense of loss which is concerned with that which we lose in our failures to come together in order to keep away evil. Indeed, the *should* here modalises the *have*, indicating the not having now of some power to act which we should have either exercised if we had it or should have tried to develop. The irreversibility that is said in the past tense for a particular event is the declaration to ourselves that we assume the obligation, not to the lost object or opportunity which we have outlived, but to the future in its wake.

'Lost' in our present situation, then, means something different from losing a possession. Our obligation requires that we hold in view the pre-existing paths which we cannot wish away but which we can strive to modify by acting collectively. Perhaps this sense is more intuitively carried in the German *los*, which carries the related meanings of 'loose', 'astir', 'wrong', 'away' and 'open'. *Los* is used in many ways, alone or as a suffix. For example, *lass mich los* or 'let me go' refers to loosening a grip. We often ask each other *was ist dann hier los?* in order to ask 'what's going on here?' or what is astir. When we ask *was ist los* it also means 'what is wrong', and the suffix means 'less' in adjectives such as *sinnlos* (senseless) or *ratlos* (without advice) and indicates privation bringing us into the ambit of evil. The loss travels into another meaning, however, when one says *los geht's!* which means 'Let's go' or 'Let's start' indicates a moment of commencement or the beginning or opening of something. The modals of lost responsibility gather all the sense at the moment of their enunciation. To be lost is to wander aimlessly and listlessly, without the means to find a way towards the ends of the world, which is our condition as the community of the forsaken.[7] The 'lost' of lost responsibilities refers to that which comes after the former is affirmed and which comes not only and not ultimately for those nearest to the loss but to everyone, because everyone is implicated in the loss of conditions of action. That we are what we are in our reciprocal gathering as the world makes each one of us responsible – obliging us to gather the power to respond – for the well-being of the gathering of the forsaken. Each decision we make either gains us more responsibilities – the power to respond – or reduces them further.

Then, the *should have* is distinguished from other past tensed modals such as *could have* and *would have* as well, and rather subsumes them in that it acknowledges that in certain cases there might have been something to be done which we did not do for whatever reasons, our own or circumstantial, that impeded us. Further, it prompts the thought of '*what should have been*', that is, it is the conditions of an action and not the individual action/s alone that should have been otherwise. Especially in the situations of evil like genocides, institutionalised racisms, and the COVID-19 pandemic, which concern the actions of supra-individual powers such as governments, corporations and global institutions, we think of what it is that prevented us from bringing about what could have been done. While in specific instances we could analyse the nature of the loss that permitted the crimes, the criticalisation of the present arrangement of the world tells us that the thing whose loss afflicts us above all is the loss of responsibility itself, that is, response-ability or the power to respond. Thus, Modals of lost responsibility problematise, in the Kantian sense, the very problematic of responsibility.

It is the very past tense in the modal of lost responsibility that bespeaks the promise and creative obligation to the future: how to imagine new ends and develop the collective means for them, and this means how to develop the collective power to do so. Rather than preaching to oneself or to others, as the *should* habitually does, the modals of lost responsibility return us to politics as the fight for freedom. As Elias Canetti remarked: 'It is the quiet, prolonged activities of the hand which have created the only world in which we care to live'.[8] Politics is today frequently mistaken for the fascist logic of friend-and-enemy but politics is the domain of the quiet, prolonged activity of the collective hands and the quiet murmur of the modals of lost responsibilities. Its time and tense are constituted by *our* sense of the foreseeable as well as unforeseeable acts and impacts we initiate and suffer. Freedom and response-ability are inseparable. To have freedom is to fight for freedoms and to create them.

NOTES

1. Translation of Paul Celan's 'Die Schleuse' by John Felstiner, *Paul Celan*, 161–162. See the insightful commentary and a different interpretation of this poem by Anne Carson, The Economy of the Unlost, 33–38, 43–44.
2. 'FÜLL DIE ÖDNIS in die Augensäcke'; Celan, *Breathturn*; my translation based on comparisons between the translations of John Felstiner and Ian Fairley, and the review of both by Charlie Louth.
3. Idyllic a priori are derivative of hypophysics; that is, a moment in the history of a few is interpreted as the natural way of being because this is the 'normal conditions of life' for them. Behind the many theories of biopolitics lie their respective idyllic a priori. Mohan, 'The Obscure Experience,' 48.
4. Further discussed in my essay 'Through the Great Isolation,' 19–21.
5. Nancy, *The Banality of Heidegger*, 37.
6. Rilke, *Selected Poetry*, 130; my translation.
7. Dwivedi and Mohan, 'Community of the Forsaken,' 31.
8. Canetti, *Crowds and Power*, 218.

BIBLIOGRAPHY

Canetti, Elias. *Crowds and Power.* Translated by C. Stewart. London: Continuum, 2012.

Carson, Anne. *The Economy of the Unlost (Reading Simonides of Keos with Paul Celan.* Princeton: Princeton University Press, 1999.

Celan, Paul. *Breathturn into Timestead: The Collected Later Poetry.* A Bilingual Edition. Translated by Pierre Joris. Apple Books.

Dwivedi, Divya. 'Through the Great Isolation: Sans-Colonial', *Philosophy World Democracy* 1, no. 1 (November, 2020): 13–21. https://www.philosophy-world-democracy.org/through-the-great-isolation

Dwivedi and Mohan. 'Community of the Forsaken'. In *Coronavirus, Psychoanalysis, and Philosophy,* edited by Fernando Castrillón and Thomas Marchevsky, 31–34. London: Routledge, 2021.

Felstiner, John. *Paul Celan: Poet, Survivor, Jew.* New Haven: Yale University Press, 1995.

Louth, Charlie. Review of *Selected Poems and Prose of Paul Celan* by Paul Celan and John Felstiner; *'Fathomsuns' and 'Benighted' (Fadensonnen and Eingedunkelt)* by Paul Celan and Ian Fairley, Translation and Literature 11, no. 1 (Spring, 2002): 123–135.

Mohan, Shaj. 'The Obscure Experience'. In *Coronavirus, Psychoanalysis, and Philosophy,* edited by Fernando Castrillón and Thomas Marchevsky, 47–51. London: Routledge, 2021.

Nancy, Jean-Luc. *The Banality of Heidegger.* Translated by Jeff Fort. New York: Fordham University Press, 2017.

Rilke, Rainer Maria. *Selected Poems of Rainer Maria Rilke.* Translated by Stephen Mitchell. New York: Vintage, 1989.

3

BADLY EXHAUSTED

Marcia Sá Cavalcante Schuback

Is it possible to speak about evil in times of pandemic? Moreover, is it possible to think of evil (*le mal*) in times of pandemic? These questions stun thus we do nothing else but to speak and think of the evil (*le mal*) of these times. Not only of the 'mal' of the malady that is spreading all over the world, but also of the evil (*au mal*) or, better yet, the evils (*aux maux*), of the world itself when the 'mal' of the malady becomes indissociable of the viralised globalisation. 'The whole world' seems to be in agreement now, because of the COVID-19 pandemic, that the world, our world, goes very bad (*va très mal*). Injustices and inequalities became even more visible and screaming. The maquinations of globalisation became even more unsustainable if the life of life shall remain alive. The control of the pandemic, that is, the 'mal' of the malady all throughout the world, coincides with the difficult question of knowing how to control the world of control that controls the world. Thus, the necessary measures to control the virus are simultaneously measures that control without measure the life of each one as well as the social lives of the world. Virus and capitalism, corona and capital, molecular and digital virus: the pandemic has rendered evident the contamination between real and virtual, confirming a cyborg-version of an alleged surpassing of the metaphysical fissure between sensibility and intelligibility, the real and the ideal, between the evil (*mal*) of matter and the good of spirit. Today, when the illness (*mal*) of the body cannot be dissociated from the illness (*mal*) of the world, when the world of each body and the spirit of the world are entirely contaminated, is it still possible to think evil (*mal*)?

One must thus begin by asking if it is still possible to think of evil (*mal*) in a time where the malleability of evil (*mal*) exhausts the worlds, the world and everything in the world, and in such a way, that it does not seem possible to exhaust this exhaustion. Can thoughts of evil contribute to exhaust this exhaustion? In its malleability, the different 'modes' of evil (*mal*) (to remember the theodician thoughts of Leibniz) are not only contaminated but also banalised: *physical evil, the 'mal'* of the physical or psychological maladies, in which we suffer ourselves, *moral evil, the 'mal'* of the psychopathy of inflicting evil upon others and *metaphysical evil, the 'mal'*, the misfortune of knowing oneself to be finite and so the enraged revolt against finitude. These three evils are intertwined. The banalisation of evil (*mal*) is not restricted to a kind of intentionality without intentionality of those who make decisions to accomplish radical evils or to an absence or emptiness of thought; the banalisation of evil is more and more connected to a 'contamination' that happens through the spectacularisation of evil, which naturalises it. All over, 'the' world regards spectacles of evil, worlds that are stuck in the evils of war and famine, in endemic and the pandemic maladies and diseases, worlds that have become coliseums of the gladiatory evil. Naturalised, the outbreak and the excess of evil do not surprise. *'Pas mal, pour un barbare'*, not bad for a barbarian, wrote Voltaire. Perhaps we should say *'pas mal, pour la barbarie du mal'*, not bad for the barbarism of evil, to make the formula a bit more actual. With the naturalisation of evil, thoughts on evil become banal by their very redundancy: the banality of evil banalises, its radicality radicalises, the privative character of evil privatises and the perversion of evil perverts. Evil, *'mal-'*, becomes the universal prefix: *malentendu* (misinterpretation), *malaise* (uneasiness), *maltalent* (misfit), *malencontre* (misfortune), *mal-être* (mal-being). It is the age of the '*mal commun*' (of common evil).

Is it then possible to think of evil in an age of 'common evil'? This question could also be asked in an inverted manner: Is it possible to think the good in the age of 'common evil'? Is it possible especially when all grand words on good and evil expose their ambiguity and hypocrisy, utilised as they are to make it public more than to legitimise the politics of death and of exploitation 'in the name of the common good'? We could undoubtedly recite the great thoughts on evil and on the good throughout different philosophical traditions; we can postulate that evil does not exist or that evil is the human. We could also do so in several ways, either to recognise our today in these thoughts or to recognise them in our today, or to not forget them or further to criticise and to add nuances to them and complement them. We can also *recite* them as Godard did in his *Book of images*, without trying to accomplish any systematisation or philosophical synthesis, for the sake of showing the resonance of that which they give us to think, in a moment of the world where thinking itself seems to have been no place in a world occupied by evil forces and deeds.

But in all of these attempts, we cannot cease to ask the question: How is it possible? How is it possible that the world has arrived at such a point? How is this malady and this malaise, this mal-being of the world possible? This question is asked even more when the reasoned responses, the hypotheses, the studies, do not satisfy the anxieties at the basis of the question, that are, in fact, the anxieties related to the possibility to end a world which makes of its end its greater finality. And not only the end of art, of god, of philosophy, of man and of the world, but the end of death. How to give an end to the politics of ends? Should the continuous assassination of the life of the world be affronted through the assassination of assassination? Should killing be killed? How can we once again find the possible in a world where the possible seems to have become impossible? The urgency to think evil is connected to the urgency to think action in relation to the action of thinking.

Everywhere today, when thinking tries to think, it finds itself in a *loop*. Because to assassinate assassination in order to save the life of life touches upon the immoderation (*hybris*) of immoderation (*hybris*) itself, on a will that is so great at controlling and mastering life that it cannot realise itself if it does not give death to death. Thus, everywhere even if in different vocabularies one of the big questions of our time is how to control for the good the control of the world and of life which is being done for the evil. How can we save the life of life if killing the killing cannot distinguish itself from killing the mortality of life and thus that which gives life to life?

This is the drama of Caligula, at least in Albert Camus' version. It is the drama of the one who violently wants the 'impossible' of exterminating the mortality or finitude of life, and for what the only possibility to accomplish it is to kill life, to destroy creation, everywhere and all the time. And not only 'in the name of' eternal life on Earth, but because of an outmost desire of 'possessing the moon', of possessing that which he has not, for a lunatic happiness of a life without the Misfortune (*Malheur*) of death, of a life without evil (*mal*). Caligula, who suffers the loss of his sister and mistress Drusilla wants to make all men happy if he could find the means of attaining the impossible – the death of death. But in order to do so, one must kill before death kills. One must advance death. One must thus employ all means to finish finitude, to take charge of a 'realm where the impossible is king'. For this, Caligula says, one must 'make laughter out of suffering' when it is possible to 'mix heaven with seas, confound ugliness with beauty', 'make sky not be sky, a beautiful face ugly, the heart of man insensible'. And as soon as Caligula hears the response of Coesonia, his wife, that 'there is good and bad, there is that which is great and that which is little, the just and the unjust', he answers:

> And I'm resolved to change them … I shall make this age of ours a kingly gift—the gift of equality. And when all is leveled out, when the impossible has come to earth and the moon is in my hands—then, perhaps, I shall be transfigured and the world renewed; then men will die no more and at last be happy.[1]

The 'gift of equality' that Caligula wants to offer to the century is the one that annuls both metaphysical differences, as those between good and evil, and cosmological, between heaven and sea. The annulation is made by means of a mixture – 'mixing heaven with sea' and through a de-realisation or des-ontologisation of beings – 'make it so that sky is no longer sky'. Caligula gets a glimpse of the realm of the impossible that is above the gods. It is an operation of disinheritance of being by which 'freedom has no more frontiers'. To the question asked by Coesonia who follows him with love: 'but if evil is already on earth, why do you want to more evil to it'?, Caligula responds that it is by a desperation that people cannot understand since they think it is a desperation caused by a malady of the soul. But for him it is desperation caused by a malady of the body, the malady of the body taken and teared off the body, from a body without body, where the mouth simultaneously tastes blood, death and fever. A desperation when, all life, as a sign of finitude, becomes repugnant. Propelled by this repugnance, Caligula wants to drive life not only to its extreme but beyond the extreme, a desire followed by total tyranny and that which, in the scenario of counter-revolution, Joseph de Maistre has described as the desire to immolate everything and see the earth soaked in blood until the extraction of all evil.[2] Driving life beyond the extreme, driving all the energy of human life to its most extreme tension – which is at the core of fascist necro-politics surpassing all frontiers, this is the 'happiness of murderers', as Caligula describes it, where it succeeds as he himself says it, to go further than the extremity of pain. For Caligula, the extremity of pain is not the death of love (of his sister and mistress Drusilla), but the fugacity of everything, including of grief and pain. It is the instant of an experience that is so atrociously fugitive that it sees the fugacity of fugacity itself: 'a devastating freedom', as he confesses. At this moment, Caligula believes to have acquired 'the divine clairvoyance of the solitary' and 'by strangling Coesonia little by little, who lets it happen without resistance', he proclaims:

> I live, I kill, I exercise the rapturous power of a destroyer, compared with which the power of a creator is merest child's play. And this, this is happiness; this and nothing else—this intolerable release, devastating scorn, blood, hatred all around me; the glorious isolation of a man who all his life long nurses and gloats over the ineffable joy of the unpunished murderer; the ruthless logic that crushes out human lives [he laughs], that's crushing yours out, Cæsonia, so as to perfect at last the utter loneliness that is my heart's desire.[3]

Caligula acquires the happiness of a 'devastating freedom' brought by the eternal solitude of man as soon as he accomplishes the isolation that only the evil of hate can accord to him. This, because the evil of hate is nothing but the 'tantalian rage' (*tantalischer Grimm*) following Schelling's expression,[4] the insurgent rage against finitude.

But facing the possibility of such a thought on evil, dramatised by Caligula, that resorbs a long history of reflection, one must still ask oneself if evil does not find itself precisely in a thought of life and existence in terms of the possible and the impossible. An entire onto-theo-philo-logical tradition that understands life as finitude and incompletion bitten by the serpent of desire of the infinite and of completion, of being-all and whole, is very well known. Schelling spoke of the anxiety of life (*die Angst des Lebens*)[5] that pushes man out from the centre inflicting upon him the wanting of returning back to this originary centre. Kierkegaard spoke of anxiety as the sault into 'the possibility of possibility',[6] the freedom that opens the edifying way of a transformation of man to become who he already is, a singular synthesis of the finite and the infinite. Thinking evil either as a decision facing the possibility of evil or facing its impossibilisation depends on a thought of finite existence as a lack of existence, as that which makes default, an existence filled with the *without (sans)*,[7] and by this, as a quest of sense. It is a thought that is itself a serpent – name-animal anagram to pensive (*serpent – penser*), that makes coincide the thought of evil with the evil of thought. Finite existence is always turned, either towards the future or the past, either towards nostalgia or redemption, seizing itself as the becoming of a past towards a future. And even when this thinking transvalorises its values and makes of finitude an infinite richness, of the default that which makes no default, it is still a strange negative greatness that defines finitude. A strange economy of the negative orients the thinking of finitude, as soon as finitude maintains itself as negative even when it is praised as positive, because it is the non-having that makes the source of the possible while infinitude, that comprehends itself as negation of finitude, maintains itself positive even when we disregard it as idealist, idealised and totalising. The infinitude, as Hegel saw it, is the positivity that can only be found as the negation of the negation. Praised as positive, negative finitude is that of the possible, of the not-yet, defined in relation to the impossible before itself. Underlining that death is the possibility of the impossibility of *Dasein*, Heidegger made it even more emphatic how impossibility remains being thought as inexistence and that the fugacity of finite existence is only seen from the perspective of the not-yet. Finite existence is thus understood as existence that is always belated in relation to a desired totality, even when this totality is conceived as a non-totalising fragment. What remains unthought, however, is the manner existence exists– the *existing while existing*, the ongoing existing, that which exceeds the linear, cyclical or even simultaneous relation between past and future.

Is it still possible to think evil at this moment of the world where existence seems to be more and more robbed of its presence? How can we respond to this question without another, which is even more significant – is it still possible to think? And moreover, what do we call thinking? And asking even further, is it still possible? Is it still? Is it the is? These questions, which we hear according to the laws of resonance, let echo the basic question of 'is it the is'? all the way to the end, to the same moment of its exhaustion and of its future of silence. It is the question that we hear a little bit everywhere – where is the *is*, in times of the bio-digital pandemic; where are we in the is, in the is-being of existence? Perhaps this question, with its metaphysical allure, has become the most physical and real question of our times. The question of where we are in the is, in the is-being of existence, this question screams and inscribes itself in each body of the world, in the whole body of the world. It is a question that is tattooed in every eye of the world, pronounced by every mouth of the world, even if we barely hear or see it. It is the question that demands from us to re-exist, touched by the *existing*, which is as inexhaustible as Rilke's flowers that grow in the middle of the tracks, without any reason to be, despite all malady and malaise of evil (*mal*).

NOTES

1. Camus, *Caligula*, 37–38.
2. Recited in the Book of Images, *Le Livre d'Images* de Jean-Luc Godard.
3. Camus, *Caligula*, 118.
4. Schelling, *Über das Wesen*, 39.
5. Ibid., 53.

6. Kierkegaard, *Samlede Vaerker*, 2012.
7. See Beckett, *Sans*.

BIBLIOGRAPHY

Beckett, Samuel. *Sans*. Paris: les Editions de Minuit, 1969.

Camus, Albert. *Caligula and Three Other Plays*. New York: Vintage, 1962.

Godard, Jean-Luc. *Le Livre d'Image*. France/Switzerland: Casa Azul Films/Écran Noir Productions, 2018..

Kierkegaard, Sören. Begrebet Angest. *Samlede Vaerker*, 1920–36, Eletronisk version 1.6, 2012.

Schelling, F. W. J. *Über das Wesen der menschlichen Freiheit*. Hamburg: Felix Meiner, 1997.

4

MIRAGES OF THE ACT

Jan Völker

In the following I would like to unfold one single point, which has been worrying and fascinating me from the beginning of the pandemic, namely the possibility of a certain illusion about our own capacity to act, which might turn into an even more effective illusion: at the end, it might look as if we would have been acting, but instead we lose the capacity to act with the growing illusion that we would have been acting.

I am not thinking of the deception, which might follow after the insight that we did not act properly or maybe did not act at all. I am not thinking of the deception from the insight that a natural force has bereft us of our capacity to act freely, that it has been dictating us how to react. What I am thinking of is an illusion, which might be called an illusion of a second degree: that we gain a raising confidence in our capacity to act freely, all the more these free acts have turned into an effective illusion. We believe even stronger in our freedom, the more it diminishes. Going through the pandemic, we might think that we actually changed the world by the way of a collective effort, but perhaps we turned the collective effort into an illusion.

I will unfold this point in three steps. First, I will point out a certain chimeric aspect of the pandemic: it displays a moment of transition, a point of conversion, which is difficult to grasp. Second, this point of conversion structurally resembles Kant's 'act of freedom' as the point of conversion between good and evil. Finally, I will propose to demarcate as 'evil' that position which pretends to be able to localise and to denominate the free act as such.

Let me begin with my first point, the chimeric, ambivalent aspect related to the pandemic and all its corresponding aspects and consequences. To be sure, this is not to say, that the pandemic in its very being is ambivalent or spectral, but it does take on a very specific phenomenal form: on the one hand, there is death, the reality and the threat of death – non-ambivalent and clear – and there are social, economic and psychosocial ruptures – some of them new, some of them simply brutal intensifications of already existent deformations. There is an abundance of data demonstrating very clearly the social, economic and psychological reality of the virus. There is an absolute clarity of facts. So, on the one hand, there is great clarity and distinctness about the effects of the virus. But on the other hand, and this is the aspect I want to emphasise here, there is a chimeric shape of this appearance, which is why I will call the pandemic a figure of transition. This chimeric figure of transition, which marks the pandemic, is a trait, which traverses the appearance of the virus in all its aspects: medical, social, discursive.

A friend of mine, the painter Mark Lammert, keeps insisting that we do not have an image for the pandemic, an image in the literal and in the symbolic sense. I think, he is right, and I think this problem of the missing image points to the problem of a missing symbol or sign for the situation we are living in. The lack of a symbol can be seen in the consequences. We are confronted with the difficulty of how to deal with the situation on various levels: how to talk about it, how to handle it, how to confront it properly, how to act and react. To effectively fight against the virus, it needs to be fought in its absence, thus we are also confronted with the mysterious absence of the threat. In conclusion, we are confronted with the difficulty to think it.

So we have a phenomenon in which death marks the end, while we are lacking the proper language to account for the situation leading up to this end. I know that a virologist might reject this hypothesis of a missing language, for they have been working endlessly to understand, read and articulate the virus. But they will also agree that the medical language does not cover the phenomenon in its entirety. The virus, as a phenomenon, indicates a transition from a purely medical phenomenon to something beyond the purely medical realm. Its effects extend beyond the medical, into the economic, the social, the psychosocial, but effectively the reality of the virus is also related to the structures of globalisation. The global and multilayered reality of the virus makes it impossible to name it within one language only, and it is here that it confronts us with a lack, the lack to coordinate the languages in which the virus needs to be named.

We cannot name what we cannot see, and we cannot see it, not because it is too small, but rather because it is present as absent: measures have to be taken against something which is not yet there, and once it is there, the measures have failed, it is too late. To be effectively fought, the virus has to be confronted in its absence. Of course, this might be said about many viruses, but here we are confronting death, and thus we are confronting death in a manner in which it can actually not be confronted, because we can only take measures as long as 'it' is not there, once 'it' is there, it is too late. Therefore, the phenomenon cannot be explained by distinguishing the medical phenomenon from its social and economic consequences: the reality of the virus is a medical as well as a social and economic crisis.

But this lack of a symbolic account does also reveal a very specific characteristic: as such a global and multilayered phenomenon, the virus points to the faculty of reason. Without reason, we cannot gain an account of the effective reality of the virus, for it is not an affair of the body, of the senses, alone. The complexity of the virus joins a moment of radical sensitivity, even its effacement in death, with a purely rational element, beyond all sensitivity, namely its absent presence. One might argue that every virus, and even every bodily phenomenon, can only be understood on the grounds of reason. Nevertheless, something is remarkable here: that we need a specific purity of reason, detached from all the effects of bodily matter, to understand the reality of the pandemic. The virus is, in part, a rational phenomenon or a phenomenon of reason.

The rationality of the virus, if I may put it like this, corresponds in a dubious way to one very specific reaction to the pandemic, which was to be witnessed especially in Germany, but also in other parts of the world: the rise of conspiracy theories to a new height. In its banality it is still odd that a phenomenon that presents a challenge to reason is provided with answers, which are precisely semblances of causal, rational answers. So we meet an old enmity: reason and the semblance of reason. With an almost perfect perversion, conspiracy theories reverse the universality of reason and seek to conflate all aspects into the specificity of one universal plot, at the end of which it is usually one person or group to be blamed. The implicit anti-Semitism turns explicit once the protestors present themselves as victims of a new regime and do not hesitate to use the symbolic image of the uniform a concentration camp inmate. The semblance of reason is not the opposite to reason, but its perversion.

A catch phrase of the conspiracy theorists is freedom: it is freedom, which is threatened and taken from them. But freedom is a keyword referred to by the measures against the virus as well. From the point of view of the measures against the virus, freedom is restricted as well, although with a different aim. So, what we find is a constellation of reason, the semblance of reason and freedom. In any case, we find ourselves in a completely Kantian setting.

The conflict in this constellation is a conflict about the question of how to act properly, how to organise our deeds. This brings us directly to Kant's discussion of good and evil in his treatise on Religion. With an opposition between reason and its corruption, circling around the notion of freedom, and taking its practical reality from our actions, the pandemic presents itself as a Kantian case.

In his treatise on Religion, Kant famously claims the human being to be evil by nature. The human being is, for Kant, characterised by a moment of an 'innate *evil*', which Kant famously calls 'radical, innate *evil*'.[1] At the same time, however, the human being has an 'original predisposition (. . .) to the good', for the human beings cannot be human beings without being affected by the moral law.[2]

Although evil is for Kant a question of our 'own *deed*',[3] he identifies a 'propensity to evil in human nature'[4] which reflects in our deeds but precedes them. The propensity [der Hang] refers to the subjective determination of the 'power of choice',[5] thus to the subjective disposition of our deeds, the basic structure of our acts, understood as a structure that precedes these acts. We might say that the propensity refers to a certain drift of our actions, a drift, which is inscribed at the ground of our actions even before they actually take place. For Kant, such an evil drift is inscribed into human nature.

But there are two different drifts to be recognised and they are both effectively inscribed into human nature. Kant calls them 'incentives'[6] [Triebfedern] and both of these incentives may inform the 'maxims' according to which we act. But we can act differently: either by following the moral law or by following self-love. On the one hand, human beings are attached to the incentive of 'sensibility',[7] simply by their disposition as natural beings, and to follow this incentive is to inscribe 'self-love'[8] into the maxims of our deeds. But on the other hand, for Kant we do also have the disposition of the moral law within us – namely as the disposition to be a rational being. We can see that the rational incentive is an exception from nature in nature: the nature of the human being is not only defined by its sensibility, but also by the exception from it.

Thus, in our acts, we have to arrange two different incentives, the incentive from our sensibility and the incentive from our rationality – or self-love on the one hand and the moral law on the other – and the propensity to subordinate the rationality to the self-love is what Kant calls the innate evil. Evil is not to be understood as a maxim itself, but is rather the way in which the two incentives are arranged and coordinated.

Thus it becomes clear that in the logical beginning there is a radical possibility of a choice, which is why Kant insists that there is 'an act of freedom',[9] which is the subjective basis of this arrangement of incentives. It is this act of freedom, which essentially marks the nature of the human being. For Kant, the nature of the human being consists in the 'subjective basis of the use of his freedom in general (. . .) the basis which (. . .) precedes any deed that strikes the senses'.[10] So there is no contradiction between freedom and nature to be found: it is the nature of the human being to make use of its freedom. We are free to be good or bad.

Finally, there is a hypothetical climax for Kant, a case of impossibility, namely to inscribe evil as a direct incentive into the maxims: that is to act for the sake of acting evil. This is what Kant calls 'diabolical'.[11] The problem here is, as it has been described by Alenka Zupančič, that this hypothetical position of the diabolic evil leads to the hypothesis that the '*diabolical evil, the highest evil, is indistinguishable from the highest good*'.[12] 'Diabolic' would be a human being who is guided by a pure evil will, by a malicious reason: a reason directed against reason. Clearly, for Kant a diabolically evil human being makes no sense: it contradicts the definition of the human being as a rational being. This is, although Kant does not put it that way, impossible.

Nevertheless, the formula of the diabolic evil points to a specific structural problem in Kant's construction, namely that good and evil intersect in their origin, which is an act of freedom. If this is the case, then good and bad are not originally distinct. As a consequence, the good act must be an act of distinction, one that establishes the human being in the distinction between the sensitive and the rational incentive. But the good act cannot refer to anything good before it takes place itself, in this sense the good act is impossible, it cannot be oriented within the possible. The evil act, then again, must be the contrary: it is that act which uses freedom to make it vanish. Kant characterises the evil act often as an act of '*corruption*',[13] it is a '*perversity* of the human heart'[14] and turns around the original disposition within the act of freedom. So we might say: the good act of freedom is an impossible act, while the evil act corrupts this act. The only way to corrupt an impossible act is to reorient it within the possible.

We can easily see now, why we can understand – within the Kantian frame – the conspiracy theories to be of evil nature, perverting the structure of reason. Conspiracy theories show us that perversion consists in an identification: they rip off the moment of transition from the pandemic and declare to know what it is and where it stems from. On the other side, the nature of the good deed is less visible. If the evil turns to the semblance of an identification, then the rational attempts to think of the moment of transition, the moment of inconceivability. The rational resists filling the lack with an image of apparent possibilities, and it tries instead to come up with a rational image, a rational symbol.

But the Kantian scenario tells us more; it is not restrained to dividing the picture into good and evil. The true problem is not the opposition between good and evil, the true problem is rather the inner corruption of the good. This problem revolves around the notion of the act. In relation to the pandemic, we might at a certain point be able to say that the virus has been defeated, and then this defeat will have been a consequence of its reasonable handling. This defeat will be a medical defeat, and it will be a rational defeat. It will be a defeat, which confines the virus in the limits of the possible, and without question this has to be considered as a good act. It is an act of freedom, a rational act.

What might get lost in this result is the inscription of the impossibility. The current measures against the virus contain moments of a proper act, for they constantly redefine the limits of the possible. To invoke just very quickly one example, just to illustrate what I am attempting to say. In the weeks before Corona, Germany had huge demonstrations by mainly young high school students, fighting against climate change. They focused a while on the international and national air traffic. But despite a very wide approval of this movement in the population, the numbers for national air traffic even went up. As an effect of the pandemic, in the recent weeks, national air traffic broke down by 99 per cent. Thus, something deemed impossible became possible.

If the virus is defeated, the world might be reset, if not use resituated in the form it had before the virus: it might be the old world, which we find to not have changed. Maybe the restitution of this world, which we would want to change, is the outcome of a true effort, of a true act at the borders of the impossible. If the world is restituted in its old form, the moment of the impossible, which tinges the act, will have been forgotten. Besides all the sad and severe effects, it might be forgotten that very simple things, which were said to be impossible, became possible within a few days. And this is the moment in which the rational answer to the virus becomes corrupted: for when we believe again that to act means to act within the possible, to secure the limits of the possible, to reinstall them once they are threatened, then we have already forgotten that acting in its true sense includes overriding the limits of the possible. The necessary act of freedom then is to insist, an act against corruption, an act within the impossible and the unknown.

NOTES

1. Kant, *Religion*, 35.
2. Ibid., p. 27.
3. Ibid., p. 34.
4. Ibid., p. 39.
5. Ibid., p. 21.
6. Ibid., p. 25.
7. Ibid., p. 38.
8. Ibid., p. 28.
9. Ibid., p. 21.
10. Ibid., p. 21.
11. Ibid., p. 41.
12. See Zupančič, *Ethics of the Real*, 79–105.
13. Kant, *Religion*, 33.
14. Ibid., p. 33.

BIBLIOGRAPHY

Kant, Immanuel. *Religion within the Bounds of Bare Reason*. Translated by Werner S. Pluhar. Indianapolis, CA: Hackett, 2009.

Zupančič, Alenka. *Ethics of the Real, Kant, Lacan*. London and New York: Verso, 2000.

5

IS EVIL AN ILLUSION?

Sergio Benvenuto

The pandemic caused by the coronavirus has sparked a debate among many philosophers as to whether this evil is entirely 'natural' or a 'social' fact (for some it is social to the extent that it does not even exist, in short, it is entirely a sham). This debate is profoundly shaped by an opposition that has a clear metaphysical origin, that between 'nature' and 'nurture', or between 'biological reality' and 'cultural product'. It is a categorical opposition that I personally reject. For this reason, I will not ask to what extent evil is natural or cultural, rather I will look at how Evil has been considered not only by our philosophical tradition but by Western culture in general.

I want to mention that personally I don't believe in either Evil or Good. In my opinion, these are allegories of our ethical judgements, which are always terribly human. I won't say anything about what *I* think evil is, but rather *how* our culture has confronted up to now the question of good and evil.

1

The Western philosophical tradition has always attempted to dismiss the belief in Evil.

Yet, surely no one can deny that the world is full of pain, injustice and evil persons. The point is the ontological status of all this misery. According to many philosophies, Evil has the status of an illusion. It would be wrong, however, to believe that this doubt concerning the existence of evil is the whim of philosophers who refuse to accept reality. For instance, even modern physics – especially Einstein – claims that time is a human illusion.

From the very beginning most of philosophical thought has postulated a close connection between Being and Good. Hence the idea that what is not Good, that is, Evil, is non-being; that non-being may appear as Being, though in fact it is not. Starting from Plato, Western thought has linked ontology to something which, in general terms, we may call ethics. In other words, it has identified a profound coincidence between what is and what is good. In Plato, τὰ εἴδη, appearances – today we would call them the *structures* – are what is truly real (ουσία). And the structure of ἀγαθόν, of Good, is the sun of the other structures, a sort of super-structure. Good is more real than any other thing. In this perspective, evil, κακόν, exists only as εἴδωλον, as semblance, non-reality, as the imaginary mould of εἶδος. Following in Platos' footsteps, Augustine also denied the existence of evil, claiming it 'exists' only as the deprivation of Good.

Spinoza argued that evil is such not with respect to the order and laws of Nature-God, but only with respect to laws governing our human nature. Deified nature is Good, only man errs, only man endures evil.

It would be wrong to view this ontological repression of evil as typical of past metaphysics, and to view that we moderns, being more courageous, would not repress it. Today many of us who claim to reject the metaphysical tradition believe, without realising it, that evil is nothing other than the shadow of Good.

We may think of the conception that dominates the Western ethical and political world today and increasingly inspires the way we conceive of democracy, human rights, free trade, etc., that is, utilitarianism. This philosophy, based on the line of thought developed in the culture that has economically and culturally dominated in the last three centuries, is defined by Bentham as follows:

> Nature has placed mankind under the governance of two sovereign masters, pain and pleasure. It is for them to point out what we ought to do, as well as to determine what we shall do.[1]

This conception has been widely criticised because it mixes what *is* (the avoidance of pain and the pursuit of pleasure) and what *ought to be* (we *ought* to avoid pain and pursue pleasure). It is said that Bentham confuses *Sein* and *Sollen* – the terms used by Hans Kelsen – 'Is' and 'Ought', merging ethics with ontology. But in fact this coalescence between 'Is' and 'Ought' is, in fact, an essential element of the utilitarian conception.

Freud turned to this utilitarian conception when he spoke of *Lustprinzip*, translated as 'pleasure principle', which I prefer to call 'desire/ pleasure principle', or even better, *lust principle*. Later Freud had to make a place for the 'beyond the *Lustprinzip*', he had to admit that it isn't true that humans tend to avoid pain and maximise pleasure, at least this is not all they do, which means they are not totally utilitarian: at least in part human beings are seduced by something that has no regard for their pleasure or pain, which means that human beings are inhabited by Evil (death drive).

2

I will not address the complex issue of whether pursuing what is considered useful conflicts with the pursuit of one's interest by others. Adam Smith's famous 'invisible hand' was theorised to explain that if and only if everyone pursues their own personal interest, the general interest will also be benefitted. The more selfish individuals are, the happier society will be as a whole (Kant's *ungesellige Geselligkeit*). Now, we know this is not true. In many miserable societies, individuals are also selfish (many are indeed corrupt) but this does not make them happy societies. Selfishness alone is not enough to build an altruistic society.

We may also ask: Do all women and men find it desirable to live in a democratic society, where civil rights are guaranteed, where women have equal rights, etc.? I have met several people who, having lived under Fascism, Nazism or Stalinism, are nostalgic for them. Back then, they say, they were happier then than today. Not just because they were young, but because when they were young they believed that the society they lived in was a happy one. In short, what makes me happy can make you unhappy, and vice versa. Over four centuries ago Etienne de la Boétie preventively questioned the 'invisible hand' when speaking of voluntary servitude.[2] That is, human beings do not spontaneously tend towards either liberty or Good, but enjoy being enslaved and adapt well to Evil.

This is why when the utilitarian West, via the Americans, defeats dictators in Iraq, Afghanistan, Libya or elsewhere, they are not always welcomed with open arms, quite the contrary. We may say that the interest of many Iraqis, Libyans, Afghans, etc., does not coincide with the ontological utilitarianism of the West.

3

We are familiar with the torment of monotheistic thought: If God can be identified with Good and Truth, how is it possible that there is so much evil on Earth, in other words how is it possible for non-truth to be true? This forces us to believe that non-being actually has a form of being – this problem arose shortly after Parmenides. In fact, I have the impression that every philosophy must address this fundamental problem: 'what kind of being is that of non-being? Are not illusions entities as well? And so on'.

This torment was later developed by Rousseau's conception, which in turn permeates Marxism and the political culture of the left. With Rousseau truth and good no longer coincide with God but with Nature. Human suffering is not caused by Nature but by human beings themselves, who, inventing society, *Kultur*, have constructed a sort of evil non-nature, which we repeatedly expose as non-truth. From culture derive private property, inequality, women's inferiority to men, etc. Rousseau further developed the Western metaphysical tradition that views evil as a human product, and specifically as a product of a humanity that has become alienated in culture. This divide between *nature* and *nurture* will permeate modern thought, from biology to philosophy. For instance, the question 'Today girls still prefer to play with dolls while boys prefer to play with swords ... is this a matter of nature or culture?' is a question that entails the fatidic distinction between sex and gender: while the first is natural, the second is a historical-social construct. According to the vision that is permeating everything today, nature is what we must return to, while culture – in particular, its economic structure – is the origin of all oppression. The ideal of a 'natural culture' stems from this vision and we take for granted it is the best, we identify it with Good (indeed: what is communism according to Marx if not the restoration of a *culture that is finally true*?). *Gemeinschaft* is a name which is given to this blessed 'natural culture'. We ensure for example that all human beings *are born* free and equal – equal with regard at least to the abilities we view as essential, namely the possibilities to learn and be good. Modernity is grounded in the myth that 'we are born free and equal' – which resulted from the combination of monotheisms and the Enlightenment. 'We are all equal' actually means 'we are all good!' Bad are those who refuse to understand that we are all good and equal – and so they deceive themselves. Like Plato, today the majority still thinks that evil is the result of ignorance. In fact, we often hear intellectuals say that the resurgence of fascisms, racisms and sovereignist ideologies is the effect of the ignorance of the masses, which means that more education is necessary to beat fascism. According to them, when fascism is not a matter of personal interests, it is about ignorance – despite the fact that some of the most prominent members of the European intelligentsia adhered to fascism or Nazism, people who certainly were not ignorant. I don't think I need to mention these people by name, since the list would be very long.

In this context, which some say is ideological, the fact that Nature shows a side that we cannot call evil (in fact, we assume that ethical judgments do not apply to nature) but, we may say, harmful, and sometimes devastating, for us, embarrasses this vision. We have seen this emerge in the wide-ranging debate that took place around the coronavirus pandemic.

4

As long as we are speaking about disasters that are not intentionally caused by humans, but closely connected to technology, such as countries polluted by dioxin, Chernobyl, Fukushima, it is easy to say, as Rousseau did criticising Voltaire: 'we were asking for it!'. However, how does one conceptualise something like epidemics, which have always existed in the world? Today, many find it difficult to accept the simple idea that nature, not having to follow any divine or human plan, has no regard for what we consider useful. That from nature we may derive also destruction. Hence the temptation to search for human *causes* – that is, human *faults* – of disasters such as pandemics, especially the one we are witnessing today. What is missing here is that humans can also be the victims of nature (as well as victims of themselves); in fact, this idea is treated as a naive illusion: humans *must be guilty* of their troubles. Humanity is *too powerful* not to be guilty.

There is an Italian expression that can be translated as 'It's raining ... thieving government!' So, this belief in the quasi-omnipotence of powerful people, with the power to make rain, is not a recent one, but an old one. In ancient Greek the word αἴτιον meant both 'cause' and 'guilt'. Also, some primitive societies (such as Jivaros in Ecuador and Peru) refuse to admit that certain natural deaths are casual: in fact, according to them they are caused by human malevolence, black magic in particular... Today's beliefs are somewhat similar. That is, we tend instinctively to identify guilt as a cause, whereby the cause of illness and death coincides with a transgression of an 'Ought to'. The meaningless indifference of nature to what we consider useful is therefore denied and pain is moralised.

This belief in the evil superpower of humans takes various forms, from the most common to very sophisticated philosophical forms, often supported by some of our most important thinkers (I would say that an almost organic function of intellectuals is to criticise the society we live in, whatever it may be. But this need to criticise one's own society often leads to disguised forms of conspiracy theories). Speaking of the reactions to COVID-19, we have witnessed typical scapegoating. China is to be blamed for the pandemic. But at a much more sophisticated level, the scapegoat is the capitalist market, techno-science, bourgeois political power, our utilitarian conception ... Some say that the global capitalist market is the cause of the epidemic because it enhances mobility. Is mobility, following the technological development of transport, a paradigmatic trait of capitalism? Certainly, fast transport is among the *causes* of the rapid spread of the epidemic today, but this cause is viewed as guilt – that of a society which one detests. 'Nature is rebelling against man' is a modern cliché. In the past it was God who caused plagues to punish us for our sins, today it is Nature.

5

The present situation highlights a strong trend in modern thought: while in the past evil was non-Being that lured man, today evil has increasingly become what defines the very being of man. On the one hand, this reversal results in a moral condemnation of humanity in its entirety, while on the other, its exaltation precisely because it is evil.

This Satanisation of humans characterises many modern philosophies, which view human subjects (not *Homo sapiens*, the biological species, but the subject that is embodied in him) as a break in the positivity of nature. Humans bring the negative into the world, and, because of this, evil. This insertion of the negative into nature is also what defines humans philosophically. Thus, Sartre conceived of the subject as a for-self – negative instance – which is opposed to each being-in-itself. Moreover, so-called post-structuralism developed the idea that language de-naturalises not only *Homo sapiens* but also nature.

It is true that the human being as ζοον λογον εχων, – an animal inhabited by language – is not viewed as the creator and master of language, given that language is the master of man (as Heidegger wrote). This is, however, in my opinion, false modesty: in fact, if it is true that language is the master of man and not the other way round, it is also true that man is *the only slave* of language. It is an extraordinary privilege. As the biblical myth says, human beings had the privilege of being the only entity to rebel against the will of God. Heidegger spoke of language as the 'house of Being', and it must be noted that houses are always human constructions.

By means of 'speaking animals' language introduces lack and absence into the world; it 'kills the thing'. We may say that this is a modern philosophical version of the myth of original sin: women and men become human by means of evil, and their becoming human generates evil in the world. Yet today this human fall corresponds to extraordinary human elevation. Today, *Homo sapiens* can claim to be proud of having been driven out of the Garden of Eden. According to this view, man's technical dominion over nature is nothing other than an extension of this original de-naturalisation of the world, which for some philosophers is consciousness (Sartre), for others language (Lacan).

Western metaphysics displays a formidable historical continuity, from the Bible of monotheisms to the modern philosophies, a continuity we may want to question, in order to interrupt it. In fact, this inviolable divide between subject and world, between culture and nature, between language and things, that has always shaped our way of conceiving of the human condition, should perhaps be rethought. We may find that the divide is not where we have always expected it to be.

6

Today Evil, brought into the world by humans by means of language, increasingly constitutes the nobility of humans, of which they should somehow be (secretly) proud.

This shift is exemplified by Goethe's Faust, whose vicissitudes open onto a modern vision of ourselves, or rather, onto the ideal of the modern intellectual elite. Modern men and women must confront Mephistopheles *continuously*. Human beings tend to describe themselves as monsters, as a *monstruum* (*monster* comes from the Latin word 'show'), as the extraordinary *show* of a void in the compactness of Being. The satanic celebration of humanness compensates the grief caused by the de-divinisation of its matrix.

It is no coincidence that modern literature, theatre and cinema, feature a series of human monsters, starting from the retroactive deification of the Marquis de Sade. Followed by Moosbrugger of Musil's *The Man Without Qualities*, Blanchot's writing on Evil and Literature, Foucault's Pierre Rivière, and finally Chigurh, in Cormac McCarthy's *No Country for Old Men*, or the serial killer of Lars von Trier's film *The House Jack Built*. The fascination that men 'beyond Good and Evil' exert on many of us today is due to the fact that the horror man once inspired in us becomes a sort of admiration for the *horrendous* character of man. (In Latin *horrendous* means horrendous the way we intend it, but also 'terribly beautiful'. The word indicated something out of proportion.) Monsters arouse an insoluble ambivalence because they show that certain humans can be totally counter-natural; however, precisely this being counter-natural renders them majestic. There is reason to suspect (few would admit to this) that Evil is the masterpiece of mankind. Hence the widespread belief that the world is in a very bad state ... Everything is getting worse. All data that point to a general improvement in our quality of life are ignored or denied. Is this bent, contrary to that of progress, something that is feared and therefore denounced? Or is it something that is secretly *desired*? Desired because we are fundamentally convinced that Evil is the truth of human beings, and that the ultimate object of human evil is man himself.

This has to do with the idea of the de-naturalisation of the world made possible by language, by *Kultur*, by neoteny ... It is a break with nature imposed by culture, the origin of all evil according to Rousseau, while in the twentieth century it is the distinctive trait not only of human uniqueness, but also of our true *freedom*. Sade's imprisonment in the Bastille and in psychiatric hospitals becomes a paradoxical testimony to the immense freedom of human beings in general.

The complete alienation of human beings from nature, by means of language and perhaps also of philosophy, therefore by means of technoscience, leads to the technological destruction of the planet and therefore of mankind, but also to a sort of desperate kind of freedom that constantly lures man, be it from a distance.

In this perspective, Good seems now an illusion, while Evil seems to reveal to us the profound truth of *Homo sapiens* as an oxymoronic, paradoxical separation from nature and from *our own* nature. This ever-increasing human exile from Being – a crime for some, a condition of freedom for others – suggests an idea not many are willing to avow: that Evil is the truth of human beings.

NOTES

1. Jeremy Bentham (1789), *An Introduction to the Principles of Morals and Legislation* (Oxford: Clarendon Press, 1907), 20.
2. Etienne de la Boétie (1576), *Discours de la servitude volontaire*. Eng. Tr. *The Politics of Obedience: The Discourse of Voluntary Servitude*, trans Harry Kurz, with an introduction by Murray Rothbard (Montréal/New York/London: Black Rose Books, 1997).

BIBLIOGRAPHY

Bentham, Jeremy. *An Introduction to the Principles of Morals and Legislation*. Oxford: Clarendon Press, 1907.

de la Boétie, Etienne. *Discours de la servitude volontaire*. Eng. Tr. *The Politics of Obedience: The Discourse of Voluntary Servitude*, trans Harry Kurz, with an introduction by Murray Rothbard. Montréal/New York/London: Black Rose Books, 1997.

Part II

WHO IS EVIL

OF HOSTS AND PARASITES

6

EVIL, TIME, HUMAN

Federico Ferrari

Having received the invitation for this meeting, I had thought about a series of questions concerning possible current and future scenarios, generated by a state of exception, seen by most as a social evil, a sort of suspension of the normal democratic life we are used to. And certainly, such an issue is important. But, then, I began to wonder more deeply about this suspension and its meaning, especially in the light of that word, 'Evil', which appeared in the title of the webinar. And so, I would like to reflect – and just to dwell – on the title of this webinar, *Is it possible to talk about evil in the era (in time) of the pandemic?* Although I understand the reasons for this title, in my opinion, the question, asked in this way, is symptomatic of an era, our era, which tends to forget or remove the dimension of Evil, and, therefore, it is a question based on an unbeatable contradiction. What is this contradiction? The thought that the question of evil is linked to time allows us to think that it is a historical condition which, as such, could be overcome by humanity and become anachronistic. It presupposes therefore that it may *not be possible*, albeit in questionable form, to speak of Evil today.

My thesis is that Evil is a condition coinciding with that of humanity and, consequently, with the question of time itself. In other words, humanity is given as the capacity of a living being to distinguish, in the temporal succession of facts, a condition called Good by its suspension, called Evil. What lies beyond good and evil is subhuman or superhuman. It is certainly no coincidence that Nietzsche linked the question of beyond good and evil to the emergence and affirmation of an *Über Mensch*, of a beyond-human, of that living being who is beyond the human. The human being, on the contrary, is that living being who, in every event of life, distinguishes and feels – since it is not a simple intellectual fact – the appearance of Good or

Evil. What does evil look like? Quite simply, as an acute form of pain or suffering, due to an interruption of a condition of balance. Evil is the lack of balance, the unbalance of the cosmos or, to put it in more contemporary terms, of the system or, in other words, of the eco-system. Human consciousness – which perceives Evil – is part of the ecosystem and, because of its consubstantial participation, can perceive the suspension of the systemic equilibrium. Man feels, through his consciousness, the balance (Good) and its suspension (Evil). In reality, we could say that man is, probably, the only living being able not only to feel part of a cosmic balance but also to feel the suspension of the balance of the ecosystem and, consequently, man is the only living being able to perceive the appearance of Evil.

Each time the flow and the balanced relationship of the parts enter into a fibrillation, a twinge penetrates the human and shows itself as an apparition of evil. Death is the representation par excellence of this breaking of a balance. Death is the suspension of the vital equilibrium of the human organism, both in its individual form (the individual) and in its collective form (humanity). The more the unbalance of the form is vast and unforeseen (e.g., as in the case of a pandemic or a massacre) the stronger is the perception of Evil. We could also say that the more death is seen as wicked, the more the balance is suddenly and abruptly disrupted. Think of Dostoevsky's unsurpassed pages on the death of a child as an emblem of Evil, as that meaningful interruption of life that sinks into the senselessness of its disappearance. The same goes for suffering as the suspension of a condition of happiness or pleasure. Suffering is the senselessness of the condition of happiness, of eudemonic balance. Once again, the interruption is Evil. This conception, under the most diverse guises and in the most varied narratives, can be found in all cultures and at all times.

Now, if it is true that Evil is situated in a trans-historic dimension of the human, it is, of course, equally true that the forms of its appearance change. Evil, in fact, is always given at a certain moment, at a certain hour. Evil is in time, just as the being of beings is in it; it is always given in a *here* and *now*, in the *da-sein*.

In this sense, the inaugural question is, for me, misplaced, because we can speak of Evil *any time*, because Evil is the rhythmic scanning, the filtering tonality that gives time to the human, just when the temporal rhythm enters into fibrillation, fractures and interrupts. Evil, then, is *in* time but manifests itself just when time is *out of joint*. One could show that time is given precisely because it can be suspended by the irruption of Evil. It is no coincidence that almost all religions place the final victory of Good as an irruption of eternity, the establishment of a dimension outside of time.

Without Evil, without its suspension, there would be no time, but only an infinite duration of Good or, better said, an unconscious quietness of itself (since Good can be perceived as Good only at the moment when it is lacking, at the instant when Evil puts it in danger).

The pandemic is a classic appearance of Evil. Not because it is the result of a wicked design but because, like all evil, it suspends a condition of equilibrium. To speak of the pandemic, therefore, is to speak of Evil.

I will not go into the form of Evil that the pandemic puts into effect. Many hypotheses have been made in recent months and, certainly, many will be made in this meeting. They are certainly all plausible hypotheses that deserve to be evaluated. I, at the moment, would not know how to add anything else, except to draw my attention and that of all of you to the need to continue to think about Evil, not only in this or that form, but in itself, in order to remain human, to avoid the risk of entering a territory, really disturbing, beyond Good and Evil, where there would remain only the pure economic management of the balance, without any interruption, painful, of the flow of life. The dream of eternity, of the Beyond Man, would be the end of the human, and, I fear, it would coincide, as many signs already presage, with the simple management of beings.

It would be a world in which the death of a child or a massacre would no longer have any chance of being a scandal, a stumble and a relative fall, but would only be part of a wider balance, certainly acosmic, economically and systemically more functional, probably anaesthetic and decidedly inhuman. To be human means to expose oneself to the experience of Evil, to expose oneself to the pain of the loss of every balance, of every sense. Only at this price can man infinitely go beyond any interruption of his identity to find himself elsewhere, that is, at the heart of himself.

7

FROM PANIC TO ECOLOGICAL IMMUNITY

Osamu Nishitani

COLLAPSING THE 'ALVEOLUS' OF OUR ECONOMIC SOCIETY

Epidemics have been around us for a long time. They even composed a part of human life, but normally spread only within a particular living area. On the contrary, the first literal 'pandemic' was the 'Spanish Flu' a hundred years ago. It occurred in the midst of World War I, first within the United States and then with the U.S. involvement in the war and with the massive movement of soldiers and other people, it rapidly spread into Europe and also into other parts of the world. At each place, it caused considerable chaos, but did not stop the World War itself, because the nation-states at war were more concentrated on combat with their military logic. In the end, more lives were lost to the pandemic than to the war.

In contrast, this time a new type of coronavirus spread into the world by the daily movement of people beyond national boundaries, united by the global economy. Our contemporary world is organised in a global economic system, driven by ceaseless techno-scientific renewals, and people were obliged to participate in it. We have to compete with each other as economic actors in the arena of the market, which increases the efficiency of this system. The political governance of each country is also conducted according to this mechanism.

Here we have to notice that the economy of our age is not mainly focused on production or manufacturing any more. The economy is now accelerated by creating consumption, in 'eliminating' or looking away from the negative aspects of manufacturing such as labour exploitation and environmental destruction. The ultimately conspicuous sector of such a consumption economy is tourism, organised as an industry. This sector does not require any manufacturing process, but the mere movement of people creates consumption. The 'pandemic' this time occurred through this movement of people, having increasingly been promoted by tourism on a globalised dimension.

At this very stage, an unknown new coronavirus (COVID-19) has emerged. Even though its toxicity is controversial, we cannot ignore the threat including its side effects: it not only causes critical illness in patients but also breaks down the whole healthcare system of the society. Because the virus is transmitted through very banal contacts among people, we need to block these and shut down our mutual contacts, in order to protect ourselves and our society from contagion. But it means a break of the very foundations of our global economic system. This reveals the fact that the system, managed by digital IT technology and functioning on the virtual, transparent plane without boundaries, relies heavily on our flesh and blood to drive the real activity. Human beings with flesh-and-blood can be infected by the virus, so all the circuits like borders, city gates, workplace meetings, entertainments and family had to be interrupted.

As is evident, this kind of countermeasure against infectious diseases, closure of meeting points and isolation of patients, has always been the same as before and there is nothing new in it. What is new is the fact that human beings cannot survive if the economic system is not maintained. Besides, it might also be new that human beings in general keep the unreasonable expectation in mind for science that a vaccine could possibly 'solve' the problem all at once.

To save the lives of people, all circulation must be stopped, which would lead to a breakdown of society. As the early reports of this virus told us, the hallmark symptom was that it collapses our alveoli. The very countermeasure against it would then, to put it metaphorically, expose us to the risk of collapsing the 'alveoli', which supply oxygen to the blood of our modern society. Therefore, our modern society has been obliged to choose between life and economy. This dilemma has caused a huge 'panic' in our society.

DISEASE AND MORTAL BODY

Although the WHO has defined COVID-19 as the epidemiological equivalent of a 'pandemic', what has happened socially has been just a panic. In fact, the confusion was caused by a crucial mismatch between the problem and the solution: contact between the virus and human beings occurs biologically, that is, at the level of cells and not of a person. These cells are the boundary between a human creature and its environment. In contrast to it, the subsistence of human beings is controlled by political administration, governed by the police or the state, city and municipality, in modern organised society. For example, since the industrialisation of society around the nineteenth century, the governance of urban communities has been constructed on the basis of population control, and people's health and sanitation have become one of major concerns and objects of control. There, groups of medical scientists have been involved in governance as experts. However, what the administration can control is only persons, not directly the micro-level contact between the virus and cells of persons.

Making up for such a mismatch, the politico-medical management resorted to the paradigm of 'control of/fight against the invisible evil (enemy)', which stemmed from the dogma of 'specific etiology' in modern medicine. They said that every disease had a specific cause, parallel to this dogma, and the idea of an immunity to viruses also started. The idea was that life was maintained by the mechanism of immunity that protected the integrity of the self. However, as research on immunity developed further, it gradually turned out that immunity could not merely be a good effect. Besides, from the side of the virus, an existence between living creature and inanimate object,[1] such an immunity meant a kind of ecological equilibrium, which is a phenomenon on a completely different dimension from that of personality. Still, from the viewpoint of medical management, such ecological phenomena tend to be kept unseen and only the aspect of 'fight against an invisible enemy' appears in front, as a matter of self-evident.

In fact, the paradigm of the 'war on terror' is closely related to the stance of medical management: in this paradigm, the health of people in a civilised society is considered to be ensured only by the extermination of the 'evil' of disease. By the same token, indiscriminate mass killing, for example, is considered as an absolute evil to be exterminated. In this way, civilisation itself is continuously maintained in the 'war on terror'. It then also becomes self-evident that healthcare management as security is a fundamental social imperative. With this understanding, the virus is targeted as a terrorist and the person infected with it has to be isolated. He/she, whether he/she is a victim or a perpetrator, will easily be treated as an 'Alien', which might otherwise be allowed only in the stereo-typed imagination of Hollywood. To repeat, it is the paradigm of medical management that makes such confusion unavoidable; even those who with consciousness of political correctness alert not to leave such discrimination on infected persons.

Further, there is one more thing to notice: economic actors are counted by numbers as a population for the governance of medical management and each actor is mostly employed by some company or a 'juridical person' (Hojin), a virtual being that does not get sick. And the modern economic system has been maintained as if it consisted of these juridical persons as standard. With this standardised virtual 'person', we might be able to switch, without problem, between real and online communications, or between 'real' work and telework. Besides, this virtual 'person' might be appropriate for working in financial markets where each deal is continuously recorded just as the change of the amount of money, or in short, numbers, which seems to require no 'real' or physical labour.

But in reality, all of these economic activities are undertaken by labouring persons. Each person is a living being with flesh and blood who can get sick or eventually starve. He/she is a real, living person who has emotions such as anger and sorrow. And it is this living, physical human being, who is attacked by the virus. Hence it is understandable that tourism which had generated consumption simply by transporting physical bodies, has been totally collapsed because of the coronavirus. Besides, the panic of our society this time has shown that our modern, highly virtualised economy is sustained in substance by essential workers, mostly with physical labours. It is all the more paradoxical that their wages do not contribute so much to the GDP or any other accountable index. Our optimistic prospect of a 'brave new world'[2] for the endless development of virtual technology has turned out not to be sustainable without such essential works of living beings.

STATE OF EMERGENCY

In this sense, our recent experience was already a 'State of Emergency'. But institutionally, it is a declaration by the government to regulate activities of individuals in the society, by releasing restrictions for executive power of the government. But then, under the state of emergency, the government must protect people's health and lives, while at the same time controlling the economic crisis, in principle. This emergency reveals the reality of a so-called free economy: no. There is no such thing as an economy 'free' from politics. In every crisis, the market requires the doping or the intervention of politics and in this sense the market economy is never autonomous at all.

By the way, as for 'emergencies', G. Agamben, taking over the thought of C. Schmitt, argued that the state governance itself is of a bio-political character and that each resort to its power is inseparable from the 'state of exception'. It may be true, but modern governance since the age of industrialisation seems to have got a different type of deployment from before: that is the 'scientific' hygiene for labourers to defend society, technically responsible for bio-politics. In this deployment, society in the sense of an industrially organised group of people emerges with the increasing importance of the economic factor in governance. And this society was formed by the motivation of political democracy.

Such an institutional deployment has continued until now and we have to make a distinction between two types of emergency: one was an emergency for power and the other was an emergency for society. In the cases of Brazil and Japan, for example, the government did not want to admit a 'state of emergency', but was obliged to declare it, because medical professionals and citizens having listened to the professionals rather claimed to have one, requiring effective and even compulsory measures to be taken, being more deeply concerned with the diffusion of infection than the government did. Isn't it a perversion?

THE CASE OF JAPAN

In the case of Japan, when the crisis of infectious disease was approaching, the government was much too anxious for the successful conduct of the Tokyo Olympics in 2020 to admit this fact, so they behaved as if the situation was not very serious. But it was a strangely unique condition of the political agenda in Japan. More fundamentally, Japan did not need to declare a 'state of emergency' at all, because the present government already had the free hand of power in place. This is indeed a peculiar situation in Japan. In a more general context, however, Japan had already experienced a common neoliberal phase of its economy for about a few decades since around the 1990s, which functioned as the basis of the audacious behaviour of our present government. In order to adapt to the global economic order, Japanese policies had reduced the scope of public administration, privatising most of the public sector into market mechanisms.

This neoliberal phase was often characterised as one of 'small government', but those who were in charge of this government fully utilised their vested interests for private gain and changed institutions to further strengthen their private interests: many people see that the Tokyo Olympics was one of the biggest examples of it. Further, these vested interests disturbed the functioning of every kind of 'check and balance' or criticism (judicial review, prosecutors, bureaucratic personnel, financial institutions, media, etc.) which had kept watching and regulating the possible risk of abuses of power. Unbearably, Japanese bureaucracy has totally corrupted into the bulwark of the Chancellor's office with the mentality of voluntary servitude, and no longer controls even the official documents. It seems to be their duty to fabricate, to hide, to destroy the archival documents or even not to record the minutes. The situation that 'power is *a priori* innocent' has almost been realised in Japan, despite its disguise of democracy, As might be well known, this was a statement by Wurtzlaf Havel who judged the Czech regime in the 1980s[3] when privatisation had penetrated all over into the area of public power.

Therefore, there was no need, no more room, for the Japanese government to issue the 'state of emergency' to expand its powers further. However, medical professionals in charge of health administration still required strong guidance by the government, because they knew that the medical system had become totally thin and slim due to the privatisation and market-based policies until then. They knew that the spread of infection could quickly overshoot the capacity of hospitals, so that it was indispensable to squeeze the number of infection tests to the minimum. (This was the main reason why the number of infected persons was so low in Japan, even though there were also many other reasons.) From this situation, it was normal citizens who mostly suffered: they were exposed to the spread of the infection, not having the possibility of getting a PCR inspection and being prevented from accessing health care in general. They also suffered economic damage. In despair, they demanded some measures be taken by the government.

In short, this means that so-called neoliberal governance, the regime that leaves everything to the market by means of all quantification (commodification), is totally incapable of responding to such a pandemic. It has only created a panic in the citizen. Citizens are human beings, not juridical persons, targeted by tiny inanimate objects.

As to the 'state of emergency', not only Japan but also many countries all over the world in general were under emergency as the 'security state',[4] being subject to the global economic order: since the declaration of 'war on terror' in 2001, preventive measures had started continuously to be taken for security, so that the distinction between war and peace had become blurred. But what is the implication then that the citizens or the society additionally called for a 'state of emergency'? It might be what Agamben called the desire to strengthen the power from below. Or I would rather see it as the demand for a 'social state', transforming the national emergency into a social emergency. It is not a demand for the defence of the state, but demand for the defence of the people themselves who form society.[5] In addition, what matters is not the so-called political system, but the administrative power and social solidarity of people. After all, Japan still keeps political democracy, just like Trump's United States does.

WHERE DID THE VIRUS COME FROM?

Modern Western medicine has got the posture to fight against Nature, in becoming a branch of natural science. And science tends to become moralised in its mission as science. In this direction, medical research and clinical medicine started combating the virus that invades the human body, by treating them as evil, rather than curing the sick patients. In this sense, it is almost inevitable that 'the war on viruses' is mentioned in medical practice, as the title of a book of overview by Roy Porter (Oxford), 'Making the Human Body a Battlefield' shows.[6] (But in the more recent case that the real fields of medicine became battlefield, it was caused by incompetent policies to leave the environment or working places for doctors and healthcare workers only as they were, which made these places into a situation like a trench.)

Anyway, as I have already mentioned, we, human beings, can control our relation to the virus, the boundary existence between living beings and inanimate objects, only ecologically, not at the cellular level. This might need a more detailed investigation on another occasion, and here I just would like to mention a few names: Tomio Tada (immunology) and Shinichi Fukuoka (life as dynamic equilibrium). Or, I would add another name, Jean-Luc Nancy, who wrote an amazing text of 'the state of exception of immunes' in the post-ontological perspective with his experience of ultimate existence.[7]

Here I would briefly explain the essence of their arguments. If the virus consists of a part of the environmental requirements for the survival of human creatures, it would be a better attitude not to fight against the virus to avoid working negatively. In fact, the term fight (war) can be employed only for human groups. Therefore, if we should falsely step into the paradigm of warfare, we would fall into a risky deviation: the research and development around viruses for prevention was inseparably connected to the area of biological weapons in the modern era. Although the medical research only aims at prevention of diseases in the cause of health and prophylaxis, the most advanced bacterial and viral research with harsh competitions is always fraught with new dangers. In this sense, research itself would become a kind of war.

The warfare paradigm is characterised by the politicisation of problems, that is, to pour the antagonism and elimination of so-called 'friend and foe' into the logical framework of politicisation. Our world is prone to this confusing politicisation, when tactical coordination and cooperation of countries is desperately needed in reality, confronting the same, new type of virus for the whole world. The WTO was supposed to be the mediator, but this organisation has continuously been exposed to pressure to politicise research for grasping the newest situation of each country. We really have to come back to the principle that the research of biotechnology, conducted 'for the goodness for humanity', cannot be justified without the collaboration and cooperation of countries across the world.

THE ECOLOGY OF IMMUNITY

In this way, the coronavirus disaster has been made into a choice between survival and health on one hand or the economy on the other. We have to say that this is the basic contradiction of the world in modern civilisation.

What then has the pandemic disclosed? It's the desperate divergence of dimensions between that of the system which drives desire, wealth and hence innovation on one hand, and that of the survival of living human beings on the other.

In the Japanese language, the word 'life' can be translated in many ways, depending on its different contexts where the word is used. In particular, the Japanese word 'seikatsu' is used for social life. It refers to the day-to-day survival of people living in a concrete environment. If we translate it back into Western languages, it would be social life or active life: if we follow the terminology of Hannah Arendt, it would be active life. It means the activity of living in society or the socialisation of living, within the texture of human relations. But this 'seikatsu' has itself been incorporated into the system of economic governance with global connections in our modern capitalism.

The entry point of each living human being to be integrated into the economic system is employment: through employment, human beings are integrated as labour force and the contractual partner is a corporation (Hojin), as we have already argued. But here we have to notice that there are two levels of integration: first, the real person is incorporated into a 'juridical person', entering into a legal relationship, then is legally virtualised and converted into something quantified as 'one' labour force. By this process, living human beings are included in the economic system, while their physical existence is in reality out of sight or at the most, as an exception. In fact, this is the 'state of exception' (ex-ception) of the economic system in modernity. This is how bio-power is exercised on each person.

In the past, the 'life' of workers was included in the industrial economic system as welfare. Welfare was built into the system itself and it was within the responsibility of the employers to maintain and reproduce this labour force. But since the economic system was reconfigured with consumption as the driving force, even the labour force became a part of capital: it began to be counted as number, the processes and contents of employment itself became a part of business, and the room for welfare disappeared. Then life has to be maintained only by the workers themselves as an expense of their consumption.

Here emerged a choice between the two, that is, survival or the economy, under the pandemic. If economic activity is a form of organisation for the common survival of human beings in general, that is, *oikonomia* or the economy in a wider sense, then people have to go out of the past economic system and open it up for the people themselves: it means to re-organise and re-combine economic activities for their own lives.

For example, Japan has to reduce economic activities just for the growth of quantitative indices, in order to survive this epidemic disaster and ensure the sustainable continuation of human society. The physical workers should be taken much more highly than before and physical constraints on the virtualisation of human activity will have to be considered much more, because we are all dependent on their essential works. Now it is no longer possible just to go back to the way things were before, as if nothing had happened. We have to re-consider and transform the whole economic system for the survival value of the people themselves.

Still, what if we should continue to maintain the illusion of prosperity (the future of civilisation)? Then social inequalities would be further widened and accelerated digital virtualisation might have a great deal to contribute to this. Then inequality would become qualitative, and the elimination of the physical would possibly cause the world to become self-extrapolating? Would it come closer to the purely digital world? No, it's sheer illusion only.

If we are to make human beings sustainable, we must at least change the mechanism of redistribution. What's more, it is important to change the system of recruitment as mass unemployment has been created again this time. It is also possible to change our modern notion of work and labour into that of activity. In so doing, we can possibly remake our society in a way that incorporates life into it. Besides, we do not need to see labour as an economic concept, but as a way of life, where working is living. The socialisation of activity, or the activity of working as it is, is to think over the possibility of 'living in the plural' or living with others. In other words, it means the re-moulding of this concept into an ecological one for humans as living beings.

As was first reflected in the 1970s when environmental pollution appeared as a problem, the pandemic should neither be reduced to a battle between nature and man, nor as a scientific and political problem. It is, as is evident, a bio-ecological problem after all.

NOTES

1. The expression, an existence between living creatures and inanimate objects, I owe to Fukuoka, *Doteki Heiko* [*Dynamic Equilibrium*].
2. Huxley, *Brave New World*.
3. Havel, *The Power of the Powerless*.
4. This point was argued by Giorgio Agamben.
5. I was inspired by Virilio, *Popular Defence*.
6. Porter, *Blood and Guts* [The title of Japanese translation is, *Making the Human Body a Battlefield*].
7. Fukuoka, *Doteki Heiko*; Tada, *Men'eki no imiron* [Semiology of Immunity]; Nancy, *L'Intrus* [The Intruder].

BIBLIOGRAPHY

Fukuoka, Shinichi. *Doteki Heiko*. Tokyo: Shogakukan, 2017.
Havel, Vaclav. *The Power of the Powerless*. New York: M.E. Sharpe, 1985.
Huxley, Aldous. *Brave New World*. London: Penguin, 1972.
Nancy, Jean-Luc. *L'Intrus* [nouvelle edition augmentée]. Paris: Galilée, 2010.
Porter, Roy. *Blood and Guts: A Short History of Medicine*. London: Penguin, 2002.
Tada, Tomio. *Men'eki no imiron*. Tokyo: Seidosha, 1993.
Virilio, Paul. *Popular Defence and Ecological Struggles*. New York: Semiotext(e), 1990.

8

LIFE, KNOWLEDGE AND FEAR IN THE CONTEXT OF COVID-19

Juan Manuel Garrido

COVID-19 faces us to the experience of fear and its critical importance in the organisation of the individual and collective life.[1] The threat of death, poverty or social disintegration associated with the current health crisis is clouding our most immediate horizons of action and understanding. It has led governments to take controversial political, economic and military or police decisions. It has sparked heated public debates and redirected a significant part of scientific research. All these transformations happen at a speed and to a degree that other recent threats have failed to generate. Even the risks related to climate change, which are far more problematic and permanent than this particular pandemic, have been unable to awake this sense of urgency. This potent yet transient evil clouds everything. It alters our cultures of health and nutrition, our professional and social life, our forms of loving, of raising, of ageing and of dying.

In this chapter, I would like to consider a specific phenomenon that the pandemic reveals in a particularly crude way: the determining role that knowledge has come to have in our social existence. Knowledge is involved in the origin, in the development and will undoubtedly be involved in the solution of the evil that we are confronting. First of all, the ability to develop tests that quickly identify the virus and the ability to generate reliable data, as well as the statistical instruments that allow us to interpret them, require very sophisticated scientific developments. Our knowledge about the disease (and our consciousness of how much we ignore of it) has had a profound impact on government decision-making, with the consequences that we know (and fear) at the level of rights and economic productivity. It is not a daring thing to conjecture that this crisis would have been extremely different if all our molecular knowledge about viruses, cells and the immune system, as well as all our knowledge enabling us to manipulate big data, had not the degree of development that it currently has. Additionally, the fact that the virus parasitised the whole global techno-economic arrangement on which our daily life rests helps to explain a great deal of the impact that it has had. Finally, all possible scenarios for overcoming the pandemic are related to research and development. It is unlikely that the authority would publicly ask for a miracle to overcome the scourge. In the Black Death, Londoners prepared by digging graves in the cemetery to help save the souls of good Christians.[2] Our interest now is to save living bodies, insofar as we know better how they work. We place our faith in human cunning.

The impact of scientific (or techno-scientific) knowledge in our world should not be measured through the supposed public preponderance of the so-called 'scientific evidence'. Today we also witness, with discouragement, how wealthy and educated nations yield to obscurantism and denial. We have seen many governments to distrust second intentions of their physicians and researchers in the context of the pandemic. We have seen them to deny unscrupulously epidemiological evidence, as much as they also have been denying evidence referring to climate change and in general to any issue in which scientific parameters would result politically and economically uncomfortable. However, none of these governments would dare to doubt that the solution to the sanitary, political, economic and social problem affecting them and affecting us all depends on a vaccine, if not on some disinfectant injection, or the use of chloroquine. It is one thing to twist public opinion with lies and denials whenever authorities perceive that it is feasible and convenient to do so. It is quite another thing to doubt seriously about the only activity that ultimately ensures the possibility of surviving, namely, R&D (needless to say, a much more lucrative activity than others, as many obscurantists surely know).

We do not understand, or we no longer understand human life as a gift (natural or divine), but as an object of production or self-production. Human beings understand they must assume the responsibility of generating by themselves the conditions of their living. The primary tool that human beings have found to fulfil this task is science and technology (although science and technology, as I will try to show later, are far from being mere 'tools' of human agency). When we are told its origins, modernity is depicted as a progressive and laborious liberation from the darkness of medieval heteronomy. Francis Bacon explicitly formulated the programme of placing science and philosophy at the service of human beings and social life. The idea that 'knowledge is power' means that knowledge about natural laws and causalities provides reliable tools for human action. According to Bacon's programme, the production of useful knowledge has to be organised epistemically as methodic research and institutionally as a social enterprise. In many senses, this programme still is in full force. It turns irrelevant how many monsters human reason will beget eventually: at present, reason has no competitors in building the world. Using knowledge in view of human life enhancement and production defines most activities in our modern societies, which for that reason have come to be known as 'knowledge societies'. As defined by UNESCO, 'knowledge societies are about capabilities to identify, produce, process, transform, disseminate and use information to build and apply knowledge for human development'.[3]

It can be reasonably asked whether science and technology effectively led us to progress or improvement in the conditions of human life. The extension of lifespan and the increase of wealth are not indisputable proofs of having reached a fuller life. What does seem much less arguable, however, is that we ended up making the production of human life entirely dependent on the production of knowledge. We have reached a point where science and technology not only, or primarily, improve living conditions, but simply make life possible. Food, health, shelter, water, energy, information, life has ceased to be viable and sustainable without maintaining or increasing the pace of research, development and innovation. In other words, the production of knowledge or 'technology at its highest level' is the force producing the minimal, the objective, the infrastructural conditions of life.[4] As German sociologist and philosopher Gernot Böhme puts it, science and technology had promised us greater autonomy and greater freedom;[5] instead, they led us to invent ceaselessly new ways of producing what before our hyper-techno-scientific age we simply 'received' from nature.

There is more to say. We have led ourselves to the puzzling situation in which there is no evil threatening life, and against which we need to deploy all our scientific and technological inventiveness, that has not been produced by the techno-scientific production of life, that is, produced exactly by the same means that produce life. Science and technology produce a form of life that is threatened by the incalculable risks emanating from the very same techno-scientific production of life. While in the twentieth century we could still link evil to human perversion or fallibility or stupidity, today not only is it uncertain what part our freedom and responsibility play in building our own good, but we also know a priori that even the best intentions, the best models and calculations, in principle and not only in fact, may have – or have already – the most destructive consequences. Our will and our intention do not control the meaning and the impact of their productions. Whether we want to admit it or not, we can no longer trust our initiative, our ability to initiate things in history.

Hence, the least we should say is that the production of life through knowledge production is far from being organised according to some shared destiny or guided by the traces of some meaningful historical horizon. Our R&D does not pursue the realisation of some ideal and ideals are no longer objective and efficient principles for individual and collective action. The production of life through knowledge is the mere production of the means of not ceasing to be alive. In other words, the end of life or life as an end is life as a means. Our life, our existence is not devoted to generating the possibility of something that we value and consider, in its turn, possible or impossible, but to generating the possibility itself as pure and simple possibility, regardless of what our decisions and actions will eventually engender and realise. Lacking purposes for the production of life implies the inability to assign limits and definition to this same production. Therefore, we may fairly call life an 'infinite' or 'unlimited' production. Life is the infinite or unlimited production of the possibility of not ceasing to be in the infinite or unlimited possibility of ceasing to be. As the French philosopher Gérard Granel states in a Seminar he gave on Gramsci in early seventies:

> None of us is worried about something more pressing than the very production of the possibility of living - the production of this possibility being what everyone pursues through the way of dressing, the relationship to money, the practice of desire or its denial, the study or the relation to the world, the political militancy or the disillusionment, etc.[6]

In my opinion, the increasing fear of global recession as a consequence of the pandemic shows very neatly up to what profound point our life has become entirely focused on producing the means to ensure the mere possibility of living. An economic crisis entails death, illness, poverty, inequality. It is an evil that deteriorates the whole life and not only parts of it. As detestable as this may appear to our intellectual sensitivity, it would be quite mistaken to disdain questions such as these: What will be in the end more painful and costly in human lives, the collapse of our health system due to COVID-19 or the planetary impoverishment that will follow lockdowns? Underestimating the fear of not receiving a salary or of losing control of your business or decreasing your capacity to consumption seems today a privilege only of those who have never experienced fear. Fear of losing your job is not the irrational dismal reaction of a salaried petty bourgeoisie sunk in neoliberal alienation, and will not disappear by enforcing rights to dignity and ensuring a minimally reasonable redistribution of wealth around the planet. Fear has its roots in the drama of life, of not ceasing to be. It is not the fear for mere survival but of being excluded from the production of life, that is from the unlimited, the insatiable production of the possibility of not ceasing to be. It is difficult to understand why we are so astonished at people's fear of globalisation and immigration. We experience serious trouble in understanding the rise of right-wing populisms, which gain ground furiously and despite destroying our dearest social values and even the rights and freedoms of the very same who support them. The fact that these populisms dominate today (as they did earlier) many societies that are at the top of the civilised world, nations with the highest levels of education and income, should lead us to wonder whether it is right to keep indulging in such intellectual astonishments. We might do better in taking note of the fact that we live in a time – not precisely a time of scarcity – when no power, no freedom, no equality, no bond, no law, no social or individual right have the least sovereignty over the infinite hunger to produce life. Then we could try to figure out whether we have the means to understand life differently.

We clearly lack the resources to understand life differently. This lack is unlikely a consequence of capitalism. On the contrary, I tend to believe that capitalism can be explained in part because of the lack of resources that Western thought developed to conceptualise life. We have been excessively focused on understanding life as an activity that is essentially productive, almost as if 'living', as well as 'being' and 'existing', were synonyms of 'producing'. This chapter is not the place to engage an exhaustive genealogy of the concept of life, although I will try to propose some indications intended to frame our philosophical discussion on the COVID-19 experience. What follows is based on Garrido.[7] I also point out that the Italian philosopher Francesco Vitale (Vitale 2018) has recently proposed a deconstruction of the concept of life by systematising, updating and extending a few proposals by Derrida.[8]

Let me start by commenting a famous phrase by Aristotle: 'the animate differentiates from the inanimate by the activity of living' (Aristotle, De anima, II, 2, 413 a 21–22). This sentence means that 'life' is an activity consisting in the production of some differentiation. The living appears as an observable natural phenomenon – think of the idea of 'vital functions' – insofar as it simultaneously indexes a difference or differentiation with respect to the dead, that is, to what the living 'is not' and endeavours not to be. A living being is a being that performs negentropic activities, that is, activities that challenge the usual thermodynamical course of things and delay disintegration. That the life of the living being consists in the production of the conditions of not dying does not mean that I am reducing life to a kind of metabolic minimum. The possibility of dying is constitutive of living beings: it is never surpassed or suppressed – unless it is also surpassed or suppressed the living condition itself. We may also define living beings as beings delivered to themselves in the task of not ceasing to be, that is, as beings essentially caring for their own being. Stones and gods do not have to deal with the problem of not ceasing to be what they are. Their existence consists neither in producing a difference with respect to death nor in identifying or being delivered to themselves in a task. It appears that the idea of living being implies the idea of self-identification, that is, of a 'self' that emerges in the task of not ceasing to be. Maybe the experience of fear is intimately locked to such self-identification. The imminence of ceasing to be, which defines life, is indexed in the experience of fear. If this is correct, then we would hardly imagine a more radical and more meaningful even though irrational experience than 'fear'. That is why Epicurus' program of achieving ataraxia by eradicating the fear of death seems so reasonable, but also so difficult to achieve.

From the fact that life is a task of not ceasing to be, a highly contradictory consequence follows for our understanding of human life – although 'human life', for human beings, frequently functions as the prototype to understanding non-human life as well (cf. Garrido 2012a). If life is being delivered to oneself in the task of not ceasing to be, then living beings want or pursue one and only one thing during their whole life: to be relieved of the task of being. Living beings are compelled to overcome and complete the lack of being that presupposes their living. They cannot not want to avoid the painful task of not ceasing to be exposed to the imminence of their death. They are compelled to escaping themselves and the living condition itself, which means, precisely, although very paradoxically, that they are compelled to ceasing to be. Life entails then, at the same time, a profoundly self-denying movement. The will to fulfil once and for all the task of being. The will to stop being the task of being. Hence, maybe, our longing for immortal life, for a life outside the order of time and space, a life without pain or pleasure, touch or relationship, a life that we could only achieve in anaesthesia or death. Life hides the will to annihilate life. Self-production in care for being leads to self-destruction. Alternatively said, self-destruction is a manner in which life fully self-produces. Life is affirmed even in death (with this formula I'd like to evoke Bataille's famous definition of erotism). From Spinoza or Kant or Hegel or Nietzsche to Baudelaire or Freud or Deleuze or Derrida, attempts at articulating this contradictory conception of life proliferate. I ignore to what extent we are caught in this contradiction, or to what extent this contradiction determines our actions. Still, I do believe that it provides a slightly less naive starting point to consider the limits of what we invoke as the meaning or the ends of life when devising a political project, installing an institution or legitimising a decision.

If knowledge is a means of life to self-produce, and life consists in the auto-immune movement of living beings self-affirming even in death, then the idea of useful knowledge, which has an enormous value to Bacon's programme as well as to our whole economic and scientific structure, as it turns so apparent today when we desperately search for solutions to the pandemic, finds severe limitations. We can put all our previous metaphysical considerations about life aside, and still note these limitations. Knowledge constantly contradicts the intentions that promote its production and transfer. Duly systematised processes of knowledge production often fail at generating useful knowledge. A large part of these processes, perhaps the largest part, either does not manage to produce useful knowledge or they produce useful knowledge in unforeseen senses and modes or for uses that were not the expected ones, in contexts that were impossible to anticipate. New knowledge does not depend upon the ends or intentions with which we generate it. Among all types of human production – except perhaps art – knowledge is the only one where the end is necessarily unknown when designing and implementing the processes of its production. And if it is already difficult to calculate the degree of usefulness for much available knowledge, it will be even more difficult for knowledge still unknown. In other words, the usefulness, uselessness or harmfulness of knowledge will always be a by-product of its production.

Hence what one might call the aporia of knowledge: on the one hand, knowledge can be used in any context and for any purpose; that is, no knowledge can prevent from being used, for the better or the worse. On the other hand, no knowledge can result from a process which would have conceived it from the start as the end of the process that produces it. This ultimately means that the unknown that structures research is completely indifferent to the existential uncertainties of human beings, and the existential uncertainties of human beings are completely ineffective in the production of the unknown. The fact is worth emphasising: a society that institutionalises knowledge production harbours at the same time, by definition or in principle and not by pathology, a non-institutional, indeed a counter-institutional component, namely, a considerable space of incertitude producing human life regardless of what we take to be the ends of human life. In a way, our entire social life seems to rest on its ability to expose itself to the unknown. But the spontaneous, the stubborn conviction that the ends of life are a matter of rational deliberation and that the means of life, mainly knowledge production, are obediently useful to our self-production, indicates to us how far are we from installing institutions capable of explicitly assuming the purpose of being exposed to what is incalculably to come.[9]

Probably the impasses of the present time stem in no negligible part from our inability to conceive our life in any other way than as a 'task', that is, as fear of not being able to honour the painful and non-chosen responsibility of not ceasing to be. It is difficult for us to escape the nihilistic crossroads in which we have been placed by our fidelity to some imaginary past or future that would be redeemed from the precariousness of living. But can we still afford to rely on imaginary worlds relieved from the fear of living? Imaginary worlds, and even the empty image that we create by only considering that everything we have is not good enough, have an incontestable force: the bloody force of denying our precariousness and of accomplishing life either in life or death. However, it seems to me that there is still so much room for something so much simpler, and maybe not so uneffective, and certainly not so costly: the fight against the poverty of our concepts to understand our ways of living.

NOTES

1. This research was funded by ANID-PIA SOC180039 and ANID-FONDECYT 1180320. The author wants to thank Nicolás Trujillo for comments to a previous version of this text.

2. Wade, 'An Unequal Blow'.

3. UNESCO, *Towards Knowledge Societies,* 318, 27.

4. Althusser, *Sur la reproduction,* 319, 251.

5. Böhme, *Am Ende des Baconschen Zeitalters*, 111.

6. Granel, *Cours sur Gramsci, Boukharine et Bordiga.*

7. See Garrido, *Chances de la pensée—À partir de Jean-Luc Nancy*; *On Time, Being, and Hunge*; and *Enamorado.*

8. Derrida, *La vie la mort.*

9. cf. Derrida, *Voyous : deux essais sur la raison.*

REFERENCES

Althusser, Louis. 1995. *Sur la reproduction*. Paris: PUF.
Böhme, Gernot. 1993. *Am Ende des Baconschen Zeitalters - Studien zur Wissenschaftsentwicklung*. Frankfurt a. M.: Suhrkamp.
Derrida, Jacques. 2004. *Voyous : deux essais sur la raison*. Paris: Galilée.
Derrida, Jacques. 2019. *La vie la mort. Séminaire (1975–1976)*. Paris: Seuil.
Garrido, Juan Manuel. 2011. *Chances de la pensée—À partir de Jean-Luc Nancy*. Paris: Galilée.
Garrido, Juan Manuel. 2012a. 'Husserl's Somatology and Life Sciences'. *Philosophy Today* 56 (3): 295–308.
Garrido, Juan Manuel. 2012b. *On Time, Being, and Hunger: Challenging the Traditional Way of Thinking Life*. New York: Fordham University Press.
Garrido, Juan Manuel. 2015. *Enamorado*. Santiago: Cuadro de Tiza.
Granel, Gérard. 1973–1974. *Cours sur Gramsci, Boukharine et Bordiga (1973–1974)*. http://www.gerardgranel.com/txt_pdf/3-Cours_Gramsci.pdf
UNESCO. 2005. *Towards Knowledge Societies*. Paris: UNESCO.
Vitale, Francesco. 2018. *Biodeconstruction. Jacques Derrida and the Life Sciences*. New York: SUNY Press.
Wade, Lizzie. 2020. 'An Unequal Blow'. *Science* 368 (6492):700–703.

9

'THE WORLD IS A VAMPIRE'

Of Pandemics and Parasites

S. Romi Mukherjee

COVID-19 has 'unmasked' the contradictions of neoliberal capitalism, contradictions which cannot be disavowed in fantasies of Occidental, European or American exceptionalism, nor covered up by the monotheistic abstraction called evil. Rather, what is of interest is how they are engendered by a global capitalism which is not necessarily neoliberal, but resolutely neo-feudal. Placed in relief is the entrenchment of a new tri-partite system whose tiers are organised through both traditional *and* biological forms of capital. And, as in the medieval period, we confront once again the extant rapport between biology and society itself. Furthermore, as Joel Kotkin observes, for many elites, COVID-19 was greeted with giddy anticipation. Rather than being a catastrophe that ruined lives, some modern clerics treated the pandemic and the lockdown as a 'test run' for the achievement of 'degrowth'. It would also serve to augment their privilege and their capacity to reproduce themselves. While the clerisy prospers, the fading middle class and the serfs are reduced to the filth of society, transformed into a paranoid and malleable population whose anxiety-ridden and abject state make them all too easy to manage.[1] However, these clerics are not known for their spiritual nobility which they dare not even feign; in truth, they are a roving band of techno-oligarchs, managers posing as politicians, malignant narcissists convinced of their innate moral superiority, junior gangsters and a new coterie of carpet baggers who, without any scruples, measure the costs and benefits of sacrificing human lives. They are catastrophe profiteers, pandemic pimps. As Marx had already noted in *Capital*, they are symptomatic of the vampire, one still thirsty and active in the new dark ages, forever reinventing itself anew.

While the vampire has existed since antiquity, it is truly born in the middle ages in synchrony with the nascent stages of capitalism. Folklore abounded with hagiographies of the revenant. Sightings were reported regularly. To be a vampire hunter was an esteemed and honourable profession. In addition, while we normally assume that vampires are bloodsuckers, during the dark ages they were also harbingers of viral respiratory illness. According to folklorist Paul Barber, the fear of the revenant was closely bound to the general fear of contagion that typified the medieval mentality.[2] Tuberculosis was also a vampiric malady and the blood that formed on the lips of the bitten was the direct result of the disintegration of lung tissue.[3] Non-biological contagions also spread and, as Jacques Le Goff remarks, the medieval world was also besieged by the 'labor pains of capitalism', where a shadow was cast over the progress of the monetary economy, a 'pre-capitalist Dracula'.[4]

The vampire feeds on the serfs, the essential workers. They are minor collateral damage in his quest to be eternal. As one who plays in shadows and light, he is the *camera obscura* that brings many to turn a blind eye to those 'workers' – code for brown, black and poor people who risk their lives for minimum wage, workers who were never really that essential, but wholly replaceable. YOLO the kids say – underneath such an affirmation is the fear that we are all not simply replaceable, but wholly dispensable. The 'workers' were already afflicted with diabetes, high blood pressure, obesity, poor mental health and asthma. For the clerisy, it is not sacrifice versus the economy. Rather, the sacrifice is good for the economy and the ultimate dismantling of the remains of the welfare state. It is a means of purging those who they despise, those who they consider the detritus and slag society. For the clerisy, poverty is not a problem to be solved – it is an aberration, a toxin, a nagging scourge, to be eliminated and cleansed from the otherwise clean and healthy system (The irony – all we talk about is the migrant, the oppressed, the refugee, but they are visible only in their deliberately engineered invisibility. The bus boy, the cashier at the supermarket, the cleaning lady, the street cleaner, the dishwasher, those other cosmopolitans who toil in the darkness.) To pastiche Adorno, the vampire is a virtuoso who animates the societal play of forces that operates beneath the surface of political forms, where 'equality' is nothing more than bourgeois ideology. But this is not a metaphor.

The vampire sucks blood, but also life-force. In ancient Hinduism, such force was called *prana*. It was associated with light, warmth, vitality and the alignment of the physical with the spiritual. *Prana* can be seized and transformed through breath. Indeed, it is through breath that consciousness finds itself transformed. In the process, all illusions (*maya*), political, personal and worldly, are unveiled and peeled away. The vampire sucks all the *prana*. He is an ideological actor and master of illusions. He is the one who makes relations of domination and hegemony appear natural and always-already there. He weaves fantastic tales of social mobility. In his love of egoism and individualism, he shatters the general intellect and the general will. All the while, he paralyses his victims with frivolous entertainment, the malaise of screens and acceleration, 'wellness', cheap knock-offs, cheap thrills and the horror of insatiable craving. He will not let you breathe (aspire).

The virus gets in your lungs. A lonely disease spawned against the backdrop of the epidemic of loneliness. London, New York, Delhi, and Wuhan, are full of lonely people. Many died alone. Expendable bodies understood only in terms of their use-by dates. Every morning we look at the 'world sick map', the 'tracker'. We analyse 'curves' and calculate the ratios of the dead, the infected and the cases . . . curves of the virus' evolution, deaths obfuscated in quantitative opacity. According to some of those who have endured severe cases, in the early stages, it feels as though hot lava is being poured down your lungs. Your body is on fire, your nose, your throat, your torso – all burning. You can only catch your breath on all fours and your hours are spent checking your oxygen, doing breathing exercises to just regain breath (not *prana*, just breath). It feels as though you are being strangled. The lungs are permanently scarred. Some victims have experienced bouts of delirium and some have claimed to have seen the devil. The virus also feeds on brains.

Eric Garner and George Floyd couldn't breathe. The latter, in his final moments, cried out:

> I'm sorry . . . I'll do anything . . . Please, the knee in my neck, I can't breathe, I can't breathe . . . I'm going down, I'm going down . . . they'll kill me . . . tell my kids I love them, I'm dead . . . you're gonna kill me man . . . Mama . . . Mama, I love you. I can't do nothing . . . please, please, please.

Garner and Floyd were victims of a pandemic. Floyd also had COVID-19. In the new dark ages, class struggle remains economic, racial *and* biological. The cops were contracted by the vampire elders. And, at the risk of repeating what is already well known – African Americans are dying from coronavirus, 2.4 times that of white Americans. Black unemployment is 35 per cent higher than that of whites. Blacks are 50 per cent more likely to be essential workers than whites, increasing their risk of being infected with COVID-19. Food insecurity has soared with one in six black families saying they are going hungry, nearly three times the rate of white families.[5]

Rage is viral too. Burnin' and lootin' is viral. Venal Vampires like Trump have been lootin' forever – extracting blood, extracting surplus labor, extracting resources, both tangible and intangible – sucking life out of the multitude. The organism, the body and the body politic were always pathological and burdened by so many original sins which keep getting passed on. There can be no reparations, nor any forgetting. Just sins bleeding out on what the philosopher Skip James called the *Hard Time Killing Floor:*

Hard times is here and everywhere you go,
Times are harder than ever been before,
You know that people, they are driftin' from door to door,
But you can't find no heaven, I don't care where they go,
People, if I ever can get up off of this old hard killin' floor,
Lord, I'll never get down this low no more,
When you hear me singin' this old lonesome song,
People,

The killing floor gushes blue-black in the Vampire's *abbatoir.* So low, progress regresses into animality at this particular end of history. So many experiments, so few foundations. A bio-socio-historical petri-dish. Sapiens. Homo Rapiens. Zero Sum Game.

And as for the future, whereas it once was an index for hope, it has become nothing more than a site of dread for the persistently traumatised. No Social Contract. No public health. You cannot reform the system. You cannot say fuck the system. We are the system – the parasite is in us. We are all complicit. As always, Samuel Beckett offers some consolation: *Ever tried. Ever failed. No matter. Try again. Fail again. Fail better.*

Quarantined – we, a species that cannot control its creations or ourselves. It came from an animal market. Some say it came from a bat. Bats carry the virus but don't get sick.

Locked down/Locked up – precisely where the story of this (the earth, humanity, society, the world), is afflicted by the something that no longer allows for the story to keep telling itself. Drop the storyline. Humanity is a fetish and species consciousness, an impossibility. And then there is the obscenity of it all – Virus porn, lynching porn, terror porn, climate porn, the spectacle of the spectacle . . . pathogens. At this particular end of history, we descend into barbarism and sloth – dopamine fiends and spectators watching our own demise.

Confined – the ambient decadence masks the contingency of things, that all is impermanent, that there is only finitude . . . that things break. To be 'crepuscular' is to also be catapulted into a certain twilight of experience. For Julien Freund, it is peoples who have disappeared, immense empires that have melted, and governments that form and exhaust themselves.[6] Civilisations are somatic and they too collapse from internal failures. Banality of the Vampire. He reappears as a daywalker at the crepuscular dawn.

Thus Nietzsche opined:

> Basic insight regarding the nature of decadence; its supposed causes are its consequences. This changes the whole perspective of moral problems. The whole moral struggle against vice, luxury, crime, even disease, appears a naïveté and superfluous: there is no 'improvement' (against repentance).[7]

Militarism, materialism, racism, poverty, capitalism, Empire, COVID, – these are not abstractions or cosmic demi-urges. They are the status quo, the causes and the consequences. The virus/vampire is a hyper-object, but beyond the object, there are real people who the virus feeds on. And we should always be on guard to avoid the theological abstraction wherein one makes appeals to the transcendent in order to naturalize the existence of hierarchical social structures on the ground. And just as we should refrain from recasting the crises of the crises in Manichean terms, let alone as some kind of 'war', we also cannot fall back into monolithic and totalizing understandings of power and domination. Among the things that have been revealed in recent times is the degree to which, on the one hand, power is powerless and how, on the other hand, institutions have very little control of the situation (crisis of legitimation). They too, like the narratives that they depend upon for their *raison d'être,* also prove to be arbitrary. Something is always slipping away. However, this is not a Foucaldian theme and variation, but rather a means of asking to what degree institutional power masks the fact that it does not exist (like the vampire). There are just winners and losers in the rigged game. The virus is the Big Other, defined too by his opacity.

Anomic wandering of the walking dead. The paucity of hope. The end is not the advent of a new beginning, but just the end that goes on. Crisis fatigue. Compassion fatigue. Herd immunity. Dashed expectations. Anomie is the general internal dis-equilibrium in the social structure, created by an over-determined set of goals and various ends of man, and an equally under-determined and de-institutionalised set of means.

In the mask, we find the dialectical image or allegorical inflection point of the hyper-object and the contradictions. In the mask, various recensions of liberty are negotiated and distilled. It becomes the symbolic nodal point for the bio-political constitution of empire and the management of populations through new carceral technologies. Masks litter the streets. Dirty masks blow in the wind. The mask is the affirmation of our participation in mass trauma. The unmasked flaunt their faux virility. The masked simulate solidarity. In the mask, the common good and personal liberty (liberty to infect) collide, security and freedom once again clash, and socialist reveries are eclipsed by the dark heart of the most toxic of liberalisms. Perhaps the mask is wrapped around Levinas's *visage* and thereby reconfigured as the new locus of the ethical encounter and the reckoning with my finitude as the finitude of the other. Or, contra Levinas, the face and the mask will no longer be the threshold of the ethical – we also do find ourselves far too exhausted to be infinitely responsible. Rather, the encounter with the other will be thickly mediated, by protective measures, the distancing of the social, and real and symbolic barriers. Moreover, the politicisation of the mask also speaks to the severing of the ethical and the political where there is no real alterity, but only those who live and those who die. The state of nature was always nothing more than the bourgeois wilderness. Global capitalism and the plagues it brings are simply conditions of 'living in the wild'.

On the first Sunday of the confinement, I looked down from my balcony in the French *banlieue* and bore witness to the last men of Europe (also known as bobos), carousing and drinking, unmasked, undistanced and unfazed. And lacking in even a modicum of self-awareness, they belted out 'Anarchy in the UK' by the Sex Pistols at their super mega Pandemic Party. *Festivus festivus* – privilege never looked so glorious. Vampires took in the view from above as the concentric circles of care collapsed underneath. Ambulances howled in the distance and news of mass graves flooded the airwaves. Refrigerated trucks rolled up behind hospitals and nursing homes. That day, an Algerian cashier at the local supermarket died of the virus, an essential worker. She lived down the street. We hadn't even hit the peak. Indecent, the last men regaled in their alternative universe. They delighted in the impertinence of their grotesque karaoke and health, which everyone was invited to watch. Toxic joy.

Next to our residence was a squat for undocumented migrant workers. As the last men sang on one side of the fence, on the other side were a group of Bangladeshis, all masked with the gloomiest of eyes, ostensibly perturbed by the racket. Victimised by the sleep merchants, they lived in close quarters, eight of them to 30 square meters. Clandestine, they worked in the black. Meanwhile, the last men sang and drank, and all they talked about was solidarity, Islamophobia and the future of the left. In private, they spoke among themselves, over craft beer, of the benefits of gentrification and its relationship to the resale value of their property. Decadence is the orgy that rages in the midst of the apocalypse, one that is fueled by yet another pandemic, that of narcissism. Melancholy at the plight of the world is, in its own way, a far more noble temperament than hedonism.

Common sense would dictate that one should never assume that their world is shared by everyone. A bit of common decency would implore one to always reflect on the stories and situatedness of those around. Empathy is not an affair of the head nor is it natural. It is a hard-learned but healthy habit. Let us recall, however, that all too often compassion finds itself impotent against the density of the suffering. The larger question concerns how to translate the body of the vampire's victim into the grounds for a historical critique of the vampire and how to dialectically invert the interpellation and the leeching with a 'counter-bite'.

Viruses are invasive and mutant intruders who come from the inside and outside of our lifeworlds. They do not emerge in vacuums, but rather, as many doctors note, they 'hijack' other cellular structures. They also mutate and thrive in relation to other viruses. Parasites cohort with other parasites and the virus enters into a secret pact with the viruses that are already pervasive in the system. Thus born is an ultra-vampire and here we evince, following Baudrillard, a new horizon of

> super conductive events . . . sudden intercontinental ravages which no longer affect states, individuals, or institutions, but entire structures, structures running across societies . . . Contagion is not merely active within each system: it operates between systems.[8]

The status quo is the fatal hyper-convergence of the paroxysm (ecological, technological, political, biological etc.). Whence the urgent need to rethink a theory of totality which engages with anonymous forms of violence and the subterranean and systemic plagues which cannot be treated as reified or given as they are embedded and viral. The idea of the totality and the idea of transformation are intimately tied. It is only by understanding the whole, of which it is a part, that theory can both understand itself and contribute to the self-understanding of something called humanity, with a view to jettisoning us out of our collective status as living hosts. What self-understanding? What does it mean to reflect on the possibility of people becoming capable of controlling their lives, as opposed to being held hostage and reduced to the harrowing struggle for survival? Is this not the definition of politics? Nevertheless, it feeds on us. We feed on it.

The philosophers of immanence have long demanded that we abandon a dualistic conception of Life. But immanence can no longer be conceived of as the ecstatic dissolution of the subject–object binary or a becoming 'water in water'. On the contrary, what we apprehend is the dark immanence of becoming 'virus in virus' (which may definitively put an end to the question of Being). And so discourses of agency are collapsed in the new ragings of rabid atomism, the vexations of virulent vitalism and the super spreader of sick organicism. The vampire is also a hydra making alliances with zombies[9] and werewolves.[10] New monstrosities will also be born. Suffice it to say, the homeopathic cure has not fared well. For the moment, we remain 'on the precipice' – of what I cannot say. And promises are rarely kept.

What of radical hope you ask? Well, let us hope that the interminable sequence of destruction and contagion that typifies our predicament may somehow be rendered creative. But beware, vampires are trans-historical creatures and there is always the risk of another wave.

NOTES

1. Joel Kotkin, 'Human Sacrifice: The Coronavirus is also Spreading a Dark New Age of Neo-Feudalism,' adapted from *The Coming of Neo-Feudalism* (New York: Encounter Books, 2020), see *The Daily Beast*, 26 May 2020, https://www.thedailybeast.com/the-coronavirus-is-also-spreading-a-dark-new-era-of-neo-feudalism
2. Paul Barber, *Vampires, Burial, and Death: Folklore and Reality* (New Haven: Yale University Press, 1988), 37.
3. Barber, *Vampires, Burial and Death*, 115.
4. Jacques Le Goff, *La bourse et la vie : économie et religion au moyen âge* (Paris: Hachette, 1997), 1–2.
5. Arun Gupta, 'How Donald Trump Killed America,' *Rawstory*, June 11, 2020, https://www.rawstory.com/2020/06/how-donald-trump-killed-america/
6. Julien Freund, *La décadence; histoire, sociologique et philosophique d'une catégorie de l'expérience humaine* (Paris: Sirey, 1984), 5–6.
7. Friedrich Nietzsche, *The Will to Power,* trans. R. J. Hollingdale and Walter Kaufmann (New York: Vintage, 1968), 25–26.
8. Jean Baudrillard, *Screened Out*, trans. Chris Turner (New York/London: Verso, 2002), 26.

9. On Zombie Capitalism, see Ronjon Paul Datta, 'Theorizing Fiscal Sacrifices in Zombie Capitalism: A Radical Durkheimian Approach,' in eds. M. Beare, S. Tombs, L. Snider, D. Whyte, *Revisiting Crimes of the Powerful: Marxism, Crime, and Deviance* (New York: Routledge, 2018), 87–110.

10. On Vampires, Werewolves, and Capitalism, see George E. Panichas, 'Vampires, Werewolves, and Economic Exploitation,' *Social Theory and Practice,* Vol. 7. No. 2 (Summer 1981), 223–242.

BIBLIOGRAPHY

Joel Kotkin, 'Human Sacrifice: The Coronavirus is also Spreading a Dark New Age of Neo-Feudalism', adapted from *The Coming of Neo-Feudalism* (New York: Encounter Books, 2020), see *The Daily Beast*, May 26, 2020, https://www.thedailybeast.com/the-coronavirus-is-also-spreading-a-dark-new-era-of-neo-feudalism

Paul Barber, *Vampires, Burial, and Death: Folklore and Reality* (New Haven: Yale University Press, 1988).

Jacques Le Goff, *La bourse et la vie : économie et religion au moyen âge* (Paris: Hachette, 1997).

Arun Gupta, 'How Donald Trump Killed America', *Rawstory*, June 11, 2020, https://www.rawstory.com/2020/06/how-donald-trump-killed-america/

Julien Freund, *La décadence; histoire, sociologique et philosophique d'une catégorie de l'expérience humaine* (Paris: Sirey, 1984), 5–6.

Friedrich Nietzsche, *The Will to Power*, trans. R. J. Hollingdale and Walter Kaufmann (New York: Vintage, 1968).

Jean Baudrillard, *Screened Out*, trans. Chris Turner (New York/London: Verso, 2002), 26.

On Zombie Capitalism, see Ronjon Paul Datta, 'Theorizing Fiscal Sacrifices in Zombie Capitalism: A Radical Durkheimian Approach', in eds. M. Beare, S. Tombs, L. Snider, D. Whyte, *Revisiting Crimes of the Powerful: Marxism, Crime, and Deviance* (New York: Routledge, 2018), 87–110.

On Vampires, Werewolves, and Capitalism, see George E. Panichas, 'Vampires, Werewolves, and Economic Exploitation', *Social Theory and Practice*, Vol. 7. No. 2 (Summer 1981), 223–242.

10

VULNERABILITY OR NAKED LIFE?

Political Imagination during the Pandemic

Tadeusz Koczanowicz

Since March we have been listening to and reading about every possible scenario of the world to come after the pandemic. No matter how diverse and contradictory these scenarios are, they have one common feature. Even when they show the world after the pandemic as being like nothing we used to know, they are all grounded in fears materialised by the social consequences of the pandemic or processes that will be catalysed by the virus and the lockdowns. Nevertheless, this fact can let us presume that during the pandemic we have learned a lot about the anxieties and fantasies of contemporary society. Therefore, possible manifestations of evil in our social life have become much easier to spot.

The text that sparked intellectual discussion of the pandemic was written in February by Giorgio Agamben, who provocatively claimed that the pandemic was invented by the government to satisfy contemporary society's need for fear, which the state uses to impose various exceptions to individual rights and personal freedoms. The pandemic for Agamben is only a replacement of the terrorist danger. From this moment on Agamben took a central part in the debate about the pandemic's social significance, warning us that what we are seeing is a fulfilment of the processes he has been depicting in modern societies for years.

The state of exception indeed became the rule as most of us were reading his 'Reflections on the Plague'. I find that this text, which is the most representative of his standpoint on the pandemic, touches on a problem that even when we disagree with Agamben – and probably most of us do – we have to face. In the very first sentence of his text he writes that his aim is to try to make sense of people's reactions to the pandemic. Avoiding this remark can cause significant misunderstanding, as Agamben was from the beginning concerned about the lockdown's consequences for our political imagination. What is more problematic is that he saw the lockdown as the outcome of the state's place in our political imagination – a testament to the fact that we can only imagine our safety as guaranteed by the institutional emanation of a community that doesn't exist and is completely abstracted from us.

The Italian philosopher points to the fact that we agreed so quickly to quarantine restrictions. For him this means that the fear fuelling the 'invented pandemic' was already with us long before the pandemic began; the plague simply materialised it. That's why we were ready to give up our daily lives, ceremonies and learning models so fast simply because our government told us to do so. For Agamben this demonstrates that today we believe only in the principle of naked life, which includes any form of community. We have no other visions of life than merely preserving our biological existence. As a result we have voluntarily given up political existence and instead chosen to become a 'fragmentary multiplicity of needy [. . .] bodies.'[1] Agamben claims that the acceptance of this existential situation will become the foundation of a new tyranny of 'the monstrous Leviathan with his unsheathed sword.'[2]

Even if Agamben's thoughts and warnings – correctly or incorrectly understood – were proven to be untrue and even dangerous, the pandemic leaves us with a series of social problems and challenges. Agamben's approach might be helpful in recognising the dynamic of people's reactions to the problems which are to come.

The main expected outcome is a financial crisis, which in a capitalist society hurts the poorest and pushes them even more out of political and public life. This problem is not limited only to economic inequalities within certain countries, but also has a global dimension between rich and poor countries and states with universal or private healthcare and democratic or authoritarian governments. In the Agambenian vision, after the pandemic we will be even more fearful and separated from one another and ready as never before to trust only those in charge of the state to protect our biological existence. This means the end of all other forms of community and the acceptance of the state's decisions as lonely individuals completely dependent on the state. No wonder some voices that appeared in the public debate during the lockdown praised the Chinese political system for its efficiency in dangerous situations.

It's worth adding that in our times 'the state' mainly refers to the nation-state, which attaches the few freedoms and rights we still have to citizenship. There are very few political attempts to solve the pandemic on a level beyond the nation-state apart from cooperation within the EU. We find ourselves in a situation when it's not even an abstract state that we can rely on, but a very precise one. This gives the state even more control because the virus knows no borders so tackling the pandemic in one state will never end the pandemic. It will stay with us as a 'foreign' danger fuelling nationalistic attitudes. The virus is a silent ally of chauvinism.

Agamben's depiction of the state is part of a debate initiated by Hannah Arendt's *Eichmann in Jerusalem*, which coined the idea of the banality of evil. While attending the Nazi official's trial, Arendt tried to understand how such an uninteresting, average man as Adolf Eichmann was capable of committing such evil deeds. Her proposed explanation lay in the bureaucratic, rationalised machine of the Nazi state, which subordinated individuals, made their moral impulses irrelevant and rendered them incapable of thinking for themselves. In Arendt's analysis of the trial, Eichmann was a typical bureaucrat who could only repeat Nazi slogans and propaganda, which he served although he didn't really hate Jews and was sceptical about those Nazi officials who did. This combined with his desperate need to be somebody important, seen in his tendency to brag about his role even when it hurt his defense (Arendt 1965). In this way Arendt painted a picture of a perfect bureaucrat who in other conditions would probably be an average employee doing an office job.

Leaders' promotion of exclusionary ideology combines with abstract efficient institutions in which individuals can't imagine an outside world or question decisions because they are unable to think for themselves to create the crossroads on which modern evil can arise.

This line of thought was also continued by the sociologist Zygmunt Bauman, who wrote about the potentiality of such evil as an inherent part of modernity. In *Modernity and the Holocaust*, he claims that the Holocaust happened in a society not different than ours with the same system of checks and balances, which were not able to prevent the realisation of the Nazi 'gardening approach' to society. The state provided the means to realise this gardening idea – not only by providing institutions but also by possessing the authority to take rights away from part of society, remove moral obligations towards certain groups and finally exterminate them; Bauman wrote:

> it took quite a few formidable modern inventions, 'rational bureaucracy' prominent among them, to render certain murders and other acts of cruelty exempt from moral judgments and so in the eyes of the

> perpetrators 'morally neutral', and to deploy a wide range of human 'values and beliefs' in the service of murder.[3]

The temptation of fetishising institutions and placing them in the centre of our worldview didn't vanish with the collapse or transformation of totalitarian states. Paradoxically it has become even stronger, since the negative example doesn't exist anymore in the popular imagination. Today, totalitarian policies are introduced as a way of solving 'refugee waves' or for 'security reasons'. In *Stranger at Our Door*, a book published several years ago as a commentary on European reactions to the refugee exodus, Bauman refers to Kant's *Perpetual Peace. A Philosophical Sketch* to note what seems obvious: that morality is universal, with *hospitality* as its major feature. Any attempts to limit morality are the opposite of morality and lead to *hostility*.

> In his *Third Definite Article for a Perpetual Peace (spelled out as* 'The World Citizenship Shall be Limited to Conditions of Universal Hospitality'), Kant insists that the issue he writes about, and what he writes about it, »is not a question of philanthropy but of right. Hospitality means the right of a stranger not to be treated as an enemy when he arrives in the land of another«. [. . .] Let's note Kant's caution – and the circumspection with which he articulates the conditions of the world – wide 'perpetual peace' on a globe on which its inhabitants 'cannot indefinitely disperse and hence must finally tolerate the presence of each other'. What Kant demands is not the cancellation of the distinction between lands [. . .] but 'a right to associate' (to communicate, to enter into friendly interaction, and eventually to try to establish mutually beneficial bonds of friendship, presumed to be spiritually enriching).[4]

In this sense the modern sovereign state is always premised on *hostility*, because it always limits rights to its citizens and often treats human rights freely. That's why Agamben calls for resigning from the concept of human rights and reinventing political philosophy by replacing all forms of subjectivity with the figure of a refugee.[5] No matter which line of thought we follow, in both cases we can say that the evil side of modernity is always present in the state and during a crisis the conditions are in favour of it taking over.

But how are we supposed to look for a different form of being together, especially now? I think that there is an aspect of anxiety connected with the pandemic that Agamben didn't take into account – the previously mentioned conviction that the world after the pandemic can't be the same. Though visions of how exactly it will look vary widely, this conviction is as strong as the fear that forces us to follow the state as the only possible way to fight for survival.

Two contradictory impulses are shaping our attitude towards the future in this moment. One is the deadly fear that Agamben sees as pushing people away from each other and making them follow the only belief left for them – the belief in naked life. This impulse leads them to support the state as the only possible safeguard of their existence. The other one is a strong conviction that the world has to change, so we have to act now in order to prevent the old mistakes from being repeated. The two impulses come from the same source and one could not exist without the other. They are much like the two drives described by Sigmund Freud in *Civilization and Its Discontents*. After the atrocities of World War I, Freud started to think that in addition to the libidinal energy which brings everything together, our culture also has a divisive force. He named the second one the 'death drive'.

During the pandemic we have all experienced death through media coverage and the situation of fear. I believe this experience has awakened the two drives, although their consequences are somewhat paradoxical. The drive of deadly fear that Agamben describes is motivated by the will to preserve biological life at the price of our political life in the community – in other words, death of the subject for life of the body.

The other impulse of new life can be depicted with reference to Jean-Luc Nancy, who in *The Inoperative Community* wrote:

> the word 'communism' stands as an emblem of the desire to discover or rediscover a place of community at once beyond social divisions and beyond subordination to technopolitical dominion, and thereby beyond such wasting away of liberty, of speech, or of simple happiness as comes about whenever these become subjugated to the exclusive order of privatization; and finally, more simply and even more decisively, a place from which to surmount the unraveling that occurs with the death of each one of us-that death that, when no longer anything more than the death of the individual, carries an unbearable burden and collapses into insignificance.[6]

In contrast to Freud, the experience of death is for Nancy an experience that transcends all differences and makes thinking about community possible, as it applies equally to all individuals. Therefore Nancy's 'communism' means overcoming death through community, which is always open.

Therefore what for Agamben is the source of a deadly community that dissolves impulses is for Nancy an existential experience that lets us think about community. During the pandemic Nancy published an essay in which she coined the term 'Communovirus' and explained that the isolation has put us in a situation that forces us to take a common stand and self-isolate, which paradoxically brings us together.[7]

What for Agamben is proof that we resigned from any form of community long before the pandemic for Nancy is the source of thinking about existential community. For Agamben, the intention to preserve our biological life by any means necessary is a sign of vanishing political life, while for Nancy it comes from the drive to preserve our uniqueness, as we can only be unique in a community. This can become the basis of the new politics. Neither philosopher is right or wrong; rather, they describe two complicated processes which are contradictory but mutually interdependent. We can only say that what is common for both processes and the philosophers who explore them is the conviction that the world can't be the same.

I think that recent events have shown us that this division – however abstract it may sound – is an accurate description of social reality in recent weeks. The first political community that has formed after the pandemic emerged in response to the killing of George Floyd. People endangered by poverty and the pandemic took to the streets to protest against the racist, structural violence of the state. No wonder that President Trump branded the 'antifa' (which is not even an organisation) as a terrorist organisation, since its main idea is to defend gatherings of people protesting for a different community from fascist and state violence. This decision didn't stop people from joining massive protests that have reclaimed public space and formed a new politics through this gesture of being together.

Judith Butler saw such situations as a source for constructing a new politics. In the contemporary United States this is a politics of memory, which is a fight to fully include African Americans in the political community. The first step is the removal of the Robert E. Lee monument in Richmond, the former capital of the Confederacy, as well as other symbols of the American state's structural hostility towards its citizens who are people of colour.

The protests also stemmed from the fact that in the United States there are economic inequalities that often correspond with racial and symbolic inequalities. People of colour are more likely to die of coronavirus and are more likely to be affected by massive unemployment. The fight for community in the wake of police violence is also a fight for equality after the pandemic.

At the same time, the Chinese government has introduced new special laws against terrorism and foreign intervention in Hong Kong that are viewed by many as another step towards imposing the authoritarian system of the Chinese mainland on the autonomous region. The announcement of the laws met with massive protests that were brutally put down by the police. The government has used anti-coronavirus laws to prosecute activists who are organising demonstrations in memory of last year's protests surrounding extradition to mainland China and the Tiananmen Square protests in 1989. The Chinese government's reaction was similar to Trump's: instead of facing the problem, they both looked for a scapegoat.

In both cases it will not work. The representatives of the state have behaved as if the only possible outcome of the pandemic were the ones that Agamben has described, while failing to take into account that divisive deadly fear is also connected to the impulse of a new community that is the source of constructing a new politics. They don't have to change the system immediately, but they will certainly change our political imagination in a way contradictory to the state's attempts to 'prepare us for self-isolation', as Agamben would say.

Judith Butler has developed a theory similar to Nancy's that can be seen as an attempt to apply Nancy's ideas to politics. In *Notes on a Performative Theory of Assembly* she writes about the irreducible aspect of the political, which she sees in the vulnerability that characterises every being and in every dependency between beings who are endangered by statelessness, homelessness or poverty. These dangers are especially strong in the unfair and unequal society we live in today. That's why she adds that precarity is a consequence of existing social structures that reveal our social nature and dependence on others. Every attempt to govern the population is usually connected with an idea of distribution of vulnerability and the decision of whose life is worth mourning. Her vision is therefore an idea of ethical commitment based in precarity.[8]

This concept can help build a new community rooted in the experience of death or vulnerability. Opposing it are the 'evil' state and populations who benefit from structural inequality and are terrified by the destruction of the symbols of its right to divide the population into groups based on those who are bound up in a system of ethical commitment and those who are excluded from it. The state and the elites will certainly try to stop the formation of such a community (or what Nancy calls communism) by every means possible, including the security argument. This doesn't mean that we shouldn't follow the WHO recommendations. It means that since the world will not be the same after the pandemic, we must find a path as individuals between deadly fear and ethical commitment to other vulnerable beings. In doing so, we can form a community that remains open while granting all beings political life.

NOTES

1. Agamben, 'What is a People'?
2. Agamben, 2020.
3. Bauman, *Modernity and the Holocaust*, 244.
4. Bauman, *Stranger at Our Door*, 73–74.
5. Agamben, 'What is a People'?
6. Nancy, *The Inoperative Community*.
7. Nancy, 'Communivirus'.
8. Butler, *Notes Toward a Performative Theory of Assembly*.

BIBLIOGRAPHY

Agamben, Giorgio. *Clarifications*, Accessed June 30, 2020 https://www.journal-psychoanalysis.eu/coronavirus-and-philosophers/

Agamben, Giorgio. *Reflections on the Plague*, trans. Gianmaria Senia, Accesed June 30, 2020 http://www.journal-psychoanalysis.eu/reflections-on-the-plague/.

Agamben, Giorgio. *The Invention of an Pandemic*, Accessed June 30, 2020 https://www.journal-psychoanalysis.eu/coronavirus-and-philosophers/

Agamben, Giorgio. 'What is a People'? trans. Vincenzo Binetti in *Means without End. Notes on Politics*, edited by Sandra Buckley Michael Hardt Brian Massumi. Minneapolis: University of Minnesota Press, 2000.

Arendt, Hannah. *Eichmann in Jerusalem. A Report on the Banality of Evil*. New York: The Viking Press, 1965.

Bauman, Zygmunt. *Modernity and the Holocaust*. Cambridge, MA: Polity Press, 2008.

Bauman, Zygmunt. *Stranger at Our Door*. Cambridge, MA: Polity Press, 2016.

Butler, Judith. *Notes Toward a Performative Theory of Assembly*. Cambridge, MA: Harvard University Press, 2015.

Freud, Sigmund. *Civilization and Its Discontents,* trans. James Strachey. New York: W.W. Norton, 1962.

Nancy, Jean-Luc. *Communovirus*, trans. Victoria Derrien, Accessed June 30, 2020 http://positionswebsite.org/jean-luc-nancy-and-shaj-mohan-our-mysterious-being/ .

Nancy, Jean-Luc. *The Inoperative Community*, trans. Peter Connor, Lisa Garbus, Michael Holland, and Simona Sawhney. Minneapolis: University of Minnesota Press, 1990.

Part III

VIRAL DISCRIMINATIONS, OR *WHERE IS EVIL?*

11

SAD TROPICS, SAD PLANET

COVID-19

Pierre Nakoulima

Translated by Chloé Pretesacque

'An evil that spreads terror round,
An evil heaven in fury found,
To scourge the crimes of nations lost to shame;
The plague – since we must call it by its name,
That in a day can glut the throat of hell,
Made war on animals, and sick they fell.
All did not die, but all were struck with death'

You will, no doubt, have recognised La Fontaine's fable 'The Animals Seized with the Plague'.

I learned this fable in college over forty years ago. It was the one that came to my mind when the virus hit Africa. I was a thousand miles away from imagining that what was only a fable would become real. Today, this fable is of unprecedented relevance and acuity.

The term 'coronavirus' is said as a singular but the event is plural as it is simultaneously sanitary, political, economic, ecological and, in our country, also religious through tradition. It made me think of Mauss's concept of total social fact, and he dared to force the COVID-19 phenomenon into a global potlatch. Everything is entangled, interwoven with the coronavirus. COVID-19 has an impact on the organisation of society in general, not a single aspect of society can escape it.

In what follows, we will look at some aspects of this entanglement.

To the Leibnizian statement that 'natura non facit saltus, nature does not make jumps' F. Warin will reply that the history of modernity seems, on the contrary, to be dominated by rare, unusual and unpredictable events.

We have been confronted to surprises, crises and traumas such as, among others and disorderly, 9/11, the Brexit, the collapse of totalitarian regimes, the Arab Spring and last in this list far, very far from being exhaustive, the coronavirus at the origin of an unprecedented upheaval of the entire planet. On cities always animated with monster traffic jams reigned a deathly silence. The virus enjoins humans, to be fundamentally relational and active, to clam up, to isolate himself, to no longer greet his fellows: a new way of life at the antipodes of what we have always known. The world that was once a global village is witnessing the withdrawal inward. The notions of borders and states are re-emerging. The coronavirus reaffirms the need of the state, the return of the sovereignty notion that the European and African unions wanted to overcome. Each nation seeks to erect ramparts around itself: it is every one for himself in the solitude of its prison. This shattering return of the state and its predominant role in managing the crisis seems to have a long-term impact on many aspects of globalisation based on the tabula rasa of political and economic sovereignty in favour of transnational firms. Resistance to neoliberal globalisation (alter-globalism) finds in the situation created by the COVID-19 arguments and motives to deepen their struggles.

Humanity is helpless facing the scale of the deaths and the speed of the virus' transmission. This pandemic highlights the excesses of this world, the excesses of a free-trade globalisation that imports and exports at all costs: viruses, populations and goods. The disease is produced by our often toxic living and feeding conditions in such a way that humanity feels overwhelmed by events and situations that it has itself produced.[1] Deforestation, urbanisation and over-industrialisation are in particular at the origin of the multiplication and mutation of microbes that cross the species barrier and thus become extremely pathogenic for humans: Ebola, SARS, Lentivirus of the macaque monkey that became HIV and perhaps COVID-19.[2]

At other times, I had considered that one could not repeat Pascal's statement that man is a thinking reed without strongly tempering it. The environmental crisis has imposed the idea of nature's fragility. This led to the argument that fragility had changed its camp. Technoscientific evolution has affirmed the power of humans. Associated with the economy, technoscience threatens to set the planet on fire if it is not already, at the Johannesburg summit in 2002 J. Chirac declared that 'the house is burning and we are looking elsewhere'. D. Bourg analyses our capacity for unequalled destruction, irreversible damages introduced into the environment since the advent of the Anthropocene.

But COVID-19 reaffirms the constitutive fragility of human being. At present we can speak of a double fragility: the originary and original fragility of man in spite of his technical power and the one of nature indebted to man's tools. But in this double fragility, that of nature is very worrying in that our capacities for destruction and nuisance exceed those of construction. That is the whole problem. In the long history of mankind, many tests revealing human frailty have been able to be and have been overcome. There is no need to recall all the ills we have faced and are facing and against which we are fighting to find solutions: malaria is endemic in many parts of the world (with 500,000 deaths a year in Africa), we live with it and we are still looking for a definitive solution.

The fragility of nature, on the other hand, is very worrying. It is a fragility that will weaken us more and more and that can make us disappear. Danger exists in the home. There is an abundance of literature on the subject.

The pandemic has brought human fragility back into focus, but it has imposed what we have been unable to do regarding the environment. Through a shock in return and as if by a 'trick of reason', as F. Warin would say, it is now the planet that breathes, Beijing that enjoys blue skies, Venice that finds its fish is freed from its 'vals'.

Now we need to contextualise the pandemic in order to make certain things obvious. Saying nothing more than what should be known and recognised, but that it is undoubtedly necessary not to presuppose that we are known by hearing what is said here and elsewhere, particularly Europe's medias.

In Africa, where religiosity, fanaticism and fundamentalism are rising up, it is very common to hear people say, as yesterday in Europe about the plague and other Spanish flues, that this is divine punishment. Accustomed to delirium, the leader of Boko haram goes so far as to thank God for this virus.

This very African attitude of seeing God everywhere is exasperating. But as Heidegger had already said, logic cannot destroy the religious but by the fact that God withdraws. But we must nevertheless keep away from the appeasement of theism. Does not the long history of humanity convince us to accept with F. Warin that our world is without God, without consolation, without compensation and without assurance of meaning? Why is it so difficult for us not to believe?

The early philosophers dismissed the Gods, to use Farrington's expression, so that a mode of knowledge, the current dominant mode, could unfold.

It is not prayers from all sides that will defeat the virus. Our traditional practitioners, with their ancestral knowledge of plants, are in the process of impressing Africa's ability to counter this virus that is driving the West crazy. The worst was foreseen for Africa. Thousands of deaths have been predicted. This could happen because of political mismanagement and the disbelief of the people. The idea of a silent epidemic can be taken seriously.

But, as always, old reflexes are resurfacing in the West when it comes to Africa, which is always seen in terms of destitution. In the case of this virus, the analyses of a certain anthropology, which are reputedly obsolete, are resurfacing. When we perceive Africa from a materialist point of view, we see nothing but lack, we hide all that is essential, especially ancestral knowledge which, in the contemporary context of universal crises, is regaining strength and effectiveness as it emerges from a long period of disregard.

By reducing everything to statistics and perceiving everything through the Western prism, under the vision of the Western system, we can allow ourselves this kind of title in *Le Figaro*: Africa's surprising resistance to the pandemic. The newspaper *Le Monde* makes its confession: the announced catastrophism, a reflection of our vision of Africa. We have forgotten that what we call grandmother's remedies elsewhere are still relevant here. University researchers associated with traditional practitioners are beginning to surprise and will surprise even more in the near future.

In the management of this crisis, particularly in Burkina Faso, there is no need to go back to what is common to the whole planet: economic, social and other aspects.

Here, one specificity stands out: it is the entanglement of the political and the traditional. The political, precisely the mayor of the capital ordered the closure of the markets, including the central market. According to the tradition of the Mosse, sources close to the elders, the central market does not close until the death of the chief of the Mosse, the Mogho Naaba. Obviously the mayor was unaware of this.

To resolve what was taking the form of a crisis between tradition and politics, sacrifices were imperative. The reopening of the large market of Ouagadougou was no longer a matter for politicians. Explanations on this aspect of the matter helped to calm the angry traders who were demanding the reopening of the market. Economic and political considerations did not triumph.

It is possible to speak here of a reinforcement of the authority of the traditionalists by COVID-19. In the end, what aspect of life escapes

COVID-19? It is this kind of questioning that allows us to come closer to Mauss's notion of total social fact.

In Africa we are facing situations that are unthinkable in the West, where we confine and deconfine, close and reopen according to the evolution of the disease and economic calculations. In this world enslaved to the religion of economics, we no longer know what the basic needs of mankind are. The race for profit has plunged the world into the icy waters of selfish calculation, to use Marx's formula.

Objectified development, as material accumulation, the result of an aspiration to well-being, seems to us in its departure to be specifically Western.

Indeed, it was in the sixteenth and seventeenth centuries that, in Europe and nowhere else, the objective and conquering subjectivity that wants to submit everything to its standards was introduced. The mathematical interpretation of nature is this revolution of thought that inaugurates modern times and makes physics, mathematics and mechanics possible. The world appears as an object on which calculating thought directs its attacks. Since Descartes, man's essential vocation has been the control, the domination of nature, which now seems to have gone out of fashion.

There is, nowadays, incompatibility between environment and development, or at least development in its present sense. Indeed, development as a Western paradigm is an enterprise aimed at transforming human relationships with each other and with nature into merchandise. It is a matter of exploiting, developing and profiting from natural and human resources. It is an aggressive enterprise towards nature as well as towards people.[3] This model of development that has dominated the planet for several centuries, causes the current social and environmental problems: exclusion, poverty, various forms of pollution etc.

Marx predicted that capitalism would create insurmountable obstacles that would lead to its loss. His predictions did not come true. But there is an urgent need to get out of capitalism. The environment has become the dead-end of capitalism that deserves to be destroyed.

In the face of globalisation, which is nothing more than the planetary triumph of the market, may we dare hope that the current health crisis, which is upsetting many of our conceptions of things, of the world and of life, will lead humanity towards a society in which economic values cease to be central, a society in which the economy is put back in its place as the simple vehicle for human life and not as the ultimate end. This means and presupposes the renunciation of this mad race towards ever-increasing consumption.[4] This is how we can avoid the definitive destruction of the environment and above all avoid the psychic and moral misery of contemporary humans. The solution lies in a diseconomisation of minds, a real decolonisation of the imaginary of the totally economic, a condition for the possibility of a world change. It is a question of putting other values, other meanings than the expansion of production and consumption, at the centre of human life.

The world must learn to renounce the economic imaginary, that is, the belief that more equals better; rediscovering true wealth in the blooming of convivial social relations in a healthy world can be achieved in frugality, in a certain austerity of material consumption.

Only Degrowth can preserve the environment and restore a minimum of social justice.

In the *Rape of the Imaginary* by Aminata Traoré, it could not be clearer: the values that humanity lacks today are non-quantifiable, non-monetisable values that do not require monopolisation and therefore induce prodigality, contrary to the fake and futile values of the liberal and neoliberal environment enjoining parsimony. These values include meaning, recognition, concern for others etc. These values are capable of founding a new culture, that of otherness at the antipodes of what liberalism serves us. It is quite simply a return to the human.

Majid Rahnema does not say anything else when he considers that the fight against what he calls 'modernised poverty', that is, the situation of being torn apart by the multiplication of one's needs and chronic insolvency, requires a sincere conversion of each one of us to a way of living, doing, creating, sharing and loving that is different. This is how

> perhaps, without giving ourselves objectives to achieve, without believing that we carry a mission emanating from our belonging to an ideology, a religion or one of the 'isms' in vogue, we would be led to participate in a much deeper movement of contagious regeneration. A movement that would move from a sincere examination of our own poverties to a way of life based on voluntary simplicity, the refusal of the superfluous and the sense of a common good that is regained and shared. From this new order of relationships with oneself and with others, alternatives could then be born, freed from the binary vision, which would aim at a return to lost balances and proportions, alternatives thanks to which a lucid and enlightened use of present potentialities (...) would perhaps be possible while respecting these balances.[5]

The basic needs of food, clothing, affection, care, love, dignity, leisure and joy are shared by all peoples and do not require the level of exploitation and accumulation achieved today by the objective development of the West.

Descartes had written 'I think therefore I am' and the 'I' had the vocation to dominate nature. This adventure has led to the modern-day 'I buy therefore I am' (as witnessed by the temples of consumption that are the hypermarkets, which would not have been depleted without the advent of COVID-19), which deserves to be relayed 'I hurt nature, I hurt others therefore I am'. Let us hope that humans will be deciliated by COVID-19 and succeed in doing so, and that we will finally leave the icy waters of selfish calculations for the warm waters of human warmth.

NOTES

1. Nancy, *Un trop humain virus.*
2. Warin, François. Notes de cours et correspondances personelles.
3. Castoriadis, *La fin de l'histoire.*
4. Latouche, *La planète des naufragés.*
5. Rahnema, *Quand la misère chasse la pauvreté.*

BIBLIOGRAPHY

Castoriadis, Cornelius. La fin de l'histoire. Paris: Du Félin, 1992.
Latouche, Serge. La planète des naufragés. Paris: La découverte, 1991.
Nancy, Jean-Luc. Un trop humain virus. Paris: Bayard, 2021.
Rahnema, Majid. Quand la misère chasse la pauvreté. Paris: Fayard, 2003.
Traoré, Aminats. Le viol de l'imaginaire. Paris: Actes Sud, 2001.

12

PHOBOS

Evil and Urgency in a Conflictual Pandemic

M. Lucía Rivera S.

In the Latin American context, and particularly in Colombia, the pandemic has shown that inequality has deepened and that the ever more unburdened action of violence and conflict (our somehow failed peace agreement, the systematic killings of social leaders and the interest of erasing history by some political factions) constitute urgent threats alongside an impoverished population and debilitated institutions. The threat of increasing an already present state of mutual suspicion and vigilance, and a tendency for justifying actions and decisions that are harmful to vulnerable individuals and groups, seems to be a disguised way of perpetuating evil in our society. Moreover, it seems that we are taking steps towards becoming a society of distrust, in which fear of contagion is mixed with diverse ways of exclusion such as xenophobia, racism, gender-based violence and aporophobia.

INTRODUCTION

The literature on evil is often centred on either the metaphysical (or theological) conditions of possibility for the existence of evil (or the radical absence of Good) or on the moral and psychological features of evil actions and agents. Though different in perspective, scope and interest, both kinds of discussions are often focused on a commitment to the relationship between agent–action–patient that presupposes or affirms the necessity of thinking in terms of individual agents and actions. However, a political view of the problem of evil seems to focus less on the intentional and 'subjective' features of evil actions and more on the structural conditions that determine the possibility of evil. In this context, evil is understood as the pernicious and damaging functioning of societies and states that preclude the possibilities of a good life for certain groups and individuals. In this sense, a theory of evil, as María Pía Lara remarks in 'Reconsidering the Perspective on Evil in the Atrocity Paradigm',[1] 'cannot be disconnected from a theory about justice, even justice is not sufficient for understanding the magnitude and the moral fracture that is produced when there have been actions that we can call atrocious'.[2]

Political evil, in its relation to injustice, features the excessive and systemic exercise of power in ways that are oppressive, cruel, humiliating and damaging to groups and individuals. The structural nature of political evil involves not only the construction and preservation of unjust institutions but also the management of social imagination and affection, the silencing of the voices of victims of evil practices and a distortion or hiding away of the plurality of histories and experiences of social and political ways of life. Political evil, then, is not merely a defective functioning of justice, either by omission or negligence but a series of active processes on different levels that configure a network of violence (both material and symbolic) on vulnerable groups. Its activity does not rest solely on the beliefs and actions of certain individuals in power, but rather on the depersonalised or decentralised cultivation of a common sense or ethos of the society at large.

In the context of Latin American politics, the deep wounds of colonisation and coloniality, along with neoliberal capitalist and patriarchal structures, give way to societies that are highly vulnerable to political evil. In the case of Colombia, the long-lasting war among the Colombian state, armed rebels, paramilitary groups, drug-lords and other factions has configured, in many ways, a culture of mutual suspicion and vigilance among citizens and between citizens and the state. This underlying ethos of distrust has been exacerbated by discursive devices that have become frequent during the pandemic, masquerading as circumstantial, while being a feature of structural injustice. I owe these categories to the women philosophers and anthropologists who have dedicated many years to the study of violence, evil and injustice from a situated and historical standpoint in Colombia and Latin America.

THE EVIL IN WORDS

Colombian philosopher Ángela Uribe Botero has studied the phenomenon of evil focusing on particular episodes of Colombian history in an attempt to frame discussions about our past through the lens of moral philosophy. In her works, she focuses frequently on the ways in which speech functions as action, serves to produce reality (or destroy it) and gives way to conditions for political agency or the denial of it.[3] One way in which evil is put into words is through a discourse that *humiliates*, this is, that excludes a group of people from the social and political community, and makes them lose control over the set of capacities and qualities for actions that they know they have.[4] Following Ernst Tugendhat, she states

> Humiliating someone, taking them (with a posture) out of the human community, is [. . .] denying them the space for mediation between that which is conditioning them and the actions they realize; in other words, it is subtracting them from the possibility of asking for and giving reasons.[5]

Humiliation is a form of evil, because the moral damage inflicted upon those humiliated is intolerable, and fractures their identity,[6] eroding the epistemic authority and self-trust required for making claims of justice.

In terms of political evil, humiliation is a feature in many of the discourses set in motion by the Pandemic, though not produced or maintained merely by it. Paternalistic attitudes towards people over seventy years of age, persons with co-morbidities, impoverished communities, indigenous communities and the Afro-Colombian population have reduced the status of citizenship of members of these groups to that of merely *patients*. In a recent statement, the vice president of Colombia referred to impoverished and vulnerable groups protesting for solutions to the dilemmatic scenario of starving or risking contagion as 'atenidos'. This is an expression that signifies someone unwilling to make their own choices and is dependent upon an authority to decide what to do, who also takes pleasure in not being responsible and living off someone else's dime. For groups that have been historically marginalised and neglected by the state, this kind of humiliating description serves to reinforce racist, classist (or aporophobic), ageist and ableist biases and to justify the lack of action by the state. It also uses the fear of contagion in order to minimise the claims for economic justice, not merely in terms of availability or access to health services but also with regard to the need for change in exploitative and unjust labour conditions.

The use and manipulation of fear of contagion also serves to transform those we supposedly fear *for* (those recognised as more vulnerable) into someone we fear *because* they are vulnerable. In Colombia, near 48 per cent of the population are called 'informal workers'. This is a euphemistic way of referring to people with no formal connection to the job market, no effective social security and scarce (if any) access to health services, who are, for the most part, people who live day to day, with no consistent or guaranteed wages. Itinerant fruit and flower vendors; people who sell gum, cigarettes, and cell phone calls; public transportation singers; car-watchers; lottery vendors; sexual workers; and countless others depend on being on the streets, risking contagion in order to be able to eat or pay for rent. The lack of institutional measures to guarantee their survival and well-being while staying at home is combined with a discourse centred on a conception of personal responsibility that inevitably frames them as dangers for society (even enemies), insofar as they are described as (or reduced to) irresponsible potential carriers of the virus.

Police brutality and excessive use of force against impoverished people trying to make a living have been exacerbated (though certainly not created) by the Pandemic, and the discourse of the irresponsible and paradoxically guilty 'atenido' has served to disguise a structural evil as a contingent and situated (and thus justified) way of dealing with the risk. But the far-reaching consequences of establishing a social imagery based on these humiliating descriptions are not trivial. The long history of conflict in Colombia and the complexities implied in the participation of many different groups with many different interests have made suspicion and mutual vigilance a staple of a culture bred in conflict. Territorial dominance has often produced informants, counter-informants and 'sapos' [snitches], and practices of inhumanity, as María Victoria Uribe Alarcón has called them,[7] such as torture and massacres as punishment for what is reported. The degradation of conflict (the inhumane, excessively cruel, disproportionately damaging forms of violence) is not merely violent against the bodies involved in the war or witnesses to it. Rather, to use Rita Laura Segato's term, they have served as a 'pedagogy of cruelty',[8] as an expressive rather than merely instrumental form of violence. It expresses the *ownership* over bodies as annexed territories; they serve as a message *from* armed men *to* other men about their capacity for cruelty and for harm. To quote Segato,

> The masculine pedagogy and its mandate are transformed into a *pedagogy of cruelty*, functional to the expropriating greed, because the repetition of the violent scene produces an effect of normalization of a passage of cruelty and, with this, promotes in people the low threshold of empathy

> indispensable for the predatory enterprise -as Andy Warhol said one time in one of his celebrated quotes: *the more you look at the same exact thing, the more the meaning goes away, and the better and emptier you feel-*. Habitual cruelty is directly proportional to the isolation of citizens by means of their desensitization.[9]

This experience of the continued spectacle of violence against marginalised, impoverished and vulnerable individuals and groups has not ceased during the Pandemic. Every day we hear and see police brutality, the demolition of homes and effective eviction of entire families in the poorest zones of the city, the continued killing of social leaders, red rags hanging from windows signalling hunger, the stranded Venezuelan migrants who cannot return to their country or live in Colombia, trans-women who are sexual workers and are left to die because the paramedics would not take them to a hospital; we hear, every day, that these measures are necessary and justified because of the urgency of decision making in light of the Pandemic. The humiliating paternalistic discourse that seems to justify this violence, and the message of ownership over vulnerable bodies, taps into an already present sense of mutual distrust and vigilance, of suspicion of those stepping out of line, of being deserving of violence. We become desensitised to it both by the fear of contagion and a cynical rhetoric by those in power.

The concept of a 'cynical rhetoric' was proposed by Colombian philosopher Catalina González in a conference in 2016. Very broadly, it served as a hermeneutical tool for analysing the ways of speaking about corruption-related crimes of the Nule brothers, that allowed highlighting their disengagement from moral considerations regarding their actions. Cynical rhetoric dissipates responsibility by way of normalising an idea about humanity in which self-interest and strategic reasoning are the central and perhaps even only relevant features of agency. In this sense, shame, guilt, commitment to values and other moral sentiments are viewed as unnecessary and a bit ludicrous. The sense in which cynical rhetoric constitutes an evil (and a political one) is that it produces conditions that make unintelligible the claims of injustice based on the experience of harm and on the moral dimensions of decisions of those in power. It claims that moral considerations are not part or should not be part of political decision making and that political matters are, for the most part, technical discussions. Starting from, but departing from González' view, I propose that cynical rhetoric not only disengages from morality and dissipates responsibility by way of ignoring moral contents, but also relates to moral intuitions and affections (mostly fear) through euphemistic substitution or platitudes. Because of limitations of space, I will focus here only on the first kind.

Euphemistic substitution is a way of masking one phenomenon in the description of another, and imposing the moral intuitions and practices that seem justified for the latter as valid for the former. The descriptions of the Pandemic as a *war* that must be won, of the virus as an *enemy* and of healthcare professionals as *heroes*, are cases of this kind of cynical rhetoric, and cannot be separated from the history of Colombia as a country in war, even if these terms are used widely around the world to describe the Pandemic. The particular character of the euphemistic substitution in the Colombian context differs from the substitution in countries where no war has been fought for decades, insofar as it does not allude to some horror far in time, lived and survived by another generation, now overcome and understood, but rather to the justification of an unending war, of an ideological opposition to the construction of peace. The use of these terms by a government that has frequently and consistently opposed the Peace Treaty with FARC, that has tried to dismantle the JEP (Special Justice for Peace), that has insisted on threatening a war against Venezuela, that calls social leaders 'vandals' and 'terrorists' is not merely accidental or innocent.

Given the history of the irregular and dehumanising armed conflict in Colombia, describing the Pandemic as a war prepares public sensibility and affections to accept innumerable deaths as inevitable, to the suspension of civil rights in the interest of security and to prioritising forceful action over care. To give an example, Amazonas, the southernmost state in Colombia, has the highest number of COVID-19 cases/million inhabitants in the country; it does not have a single ICU unit and can only be accessed by plane. The historical negligence of the state towards the region and the twenty-six indigenous communities that inhabit it reflects on the high death rate and the disproportionate contagion of indigenous people. When health care professionals in Amazonas asked the government for help because of the dire conditions for caring for patients (no ventilators, no face masks, health professionals dressed in garbage bags for lack of protective suits), the response was aligned with the description of a war: along with supplies and medical staff, one thousand soldiers in *Tyvek* suits, masks, boots, gloves and fully armed were deployed in order to contain the virus and the population. The idea of war in Colombia is tied to the impression that the presence of the state is mostly (or merely) a military presence; it gives way to the normalisation of the notion that enforcing the law (or public health recommendations) with combat weapons is justifiable.

Heroes are expected to give their lives in the fight, to leave family and friends behind, to put their bodies in the line of fire. In the first version of Presidential Decree 538 of 12 April 2020, all health care professionals were called to service with 'obligatory compliance', much like a military draft. At the moment, neither the state nor the private employers of healthcare professionals were providing bio-security equipment (masks, gloves, suits) and health insurance companies rejected to consider contagion with COVID-19 as an occupational illness. Viewing doctors and nurses as heroes allowed for reconciling the precarious conditions for their work and the thankful applause from balconies with sacrificing themselves. Their claims of unjust contracts and wages, inadequate equipment, of the unnecessary harm they were being exposed to, were silenced by the euphemistic substitution of 'healthcare professional' for 'hero'.

Viewing the virus as an enemy inserts itself into the narrative of war and displaces all other concerns as secondary to the victory over it. The long-lasting Colombian war has served right-wing governments as a justification for neglecting (and actively destructing) the public educational and health systems, social security, environments, ecosystems, cultures, and human rights. It has been a justification for censure, spying, unlawful detention and more. Certain contingency measures during the Pandemic have deepened not only economic inequality, but have also promoted symbolic injustices,[10] the arbitrary requirement of sensible data and monitoring by employers, health and insurance companies, local governments, and others. In the logic of an irregular internal war, the enemy is not clearly visible, not entirely discernible; any one of us might be an embodiment of the enemy, must be watched out for, and fall under the authority of the State. As I stated before, when talking about humiliating discourses, the substitution of persons for potential carriers or for merely numbers in a chart serves to promote an ethos of distrust and constant fear that is ultimately desensitising to systemic oppression, cruelty and other forms of political evil.

NOTES

1. Uribe Botero & de Gamboa Tapias, eds., *Fuentes del mal*, 145–171
2. Ibid., 146. All quotes are originally in Spanish and have been translated by me.
3. Cf. Uribe Botero, 'El mal en las palabras. "El hombre tempestad"', 100–101.
4. Cf. Uribe Botero, *Perfiles del mal en la historia de Colombia*, 30–31.
5. Ibid., (ibid., 37).
6. Cf. Lara, in Uribe Botero & de Gamboa Tapias, *Fuentes del mal*, 152 n.

7. Cf. Uribe Alarcón, *Antropología de la inhumanidad.*
8. Cf. Segato, *Narrar el mal,* 13–33.
9. Ibid., 19–20.
10. One example is 'Pico y género', a policy for regulating the number of people in public spaces, which gave permission for going out on certain days or hours according to a person's gender or their sex as indicated in their ID. In Bogotá and other cities a rise in violence against trans- and non-binary people was reported perpetuated both by Police officers and by civilians. Insults, harassment, beatings and unlawful arrests were reported. After great uproar in social networks and a 'tutelatón' (Tutela is the right to sue the State for violating basic rights), some governors and mayors withdrew the measure entirely or the requirement of sex indicated in the ID.

REFERENCES

Lara, María Pía (2009). *Narrar el mal.* Barcelona: Gedisa.

Segato, Rita Laura (2018). *La guerra contra las mujeres.* Buenos Aires: Prometeo Libros.

Uribe Alarcón, María Victoria (2015). *Hilando fino. Voces femeninas en La Violencia.* Bogotá: Editorial Universidad del Rosario.

Uribe Alarcón, María Victoria (2018). *Antropología de la inhumanidad. Un ensayo interpretativo sobre el Terror en Colombia.* 2da Edición. Bogotá: Editorial Universidad de los Andes.

Uribe Botero, Ángela (2009). *Perfiles del mal en la historia de Colombia.* Bogotá: Universidad Nacional de Colombia.

Uribe Botero, Ángela (2009a). 'El mal en las palabras. "El hombre tempestad"'. *Estudios Políticos* 34: 97–111.

Uribe Botero, Ángela and de Gamboa Tapias, Camila (eds.) (2012). *Fuentes del mal.* Bogotá: Universidad Nacional de Colombia, Editorial Universidad del Rosario.

13

IT WOULD BE NICE TO TESTIFY THAT WE ARE AWARE OF OUR NIGHT

Parham Shahrjerdi

Translated by Chloé Pretesacque

I must start with a confession: for this intervention, I had written pages and pages. And then I fell ill. Something vital was missing. I had talked about COVID-19. But the pages were inert. Nothing was moving, nothing was emerging, nothing was alive. Something was missing. The heart was missing. Because it wasn't all about COVID-19. And then I remembered this line by Jean Racine: my evil comes from further away. I had to bring up the past. Older than COVID. Deadlier than a virus.

Is it really possible to talk about COVID-19 in the same way everywhere in the world?

In what context, under what regime does the virus actually arise?

I will elaborate in a moment. Before I do so, I would like to enunciate that this space that has been given to me by you, I do not want to keep it for myself. I want to put it at the service of those whom I call the invisible people. Those who are never there, those who are no longer there. Those who have no right to speak.

So I am going to speak about them, here, in French. In a language that is foreign to them. Here, in France. In a country that is foreign to them. Yes, to speak about Iran is to make present this elsewhere that eludes us. To give a voice, to give life, to what remains silent, to what fades away.

So I asked the question earlier: Under what regime is this virus emerging?

In Iran. Iran is far away. It is falsely within reach. It is far from our knowledge, far from our lifestyle, far from our laws, our rules, our fears. Iran is a two-and-a-half-hour time difference, and a geographical distance of more than 5,000 kilometers. So you see, to talk about Iran, one has to lose one's bearings, one's certainties. So for a few minutes, let's leave aside what's going on here.

For the longest time, it was difficult to talk about Iran. We used to say: ah, yes, the poor Iranians, how they suffer! Without ever putting oneself in their shoes. Their plight was far away, unapproachable. Today, a few hundred thousand deaths later, we are beginning to see clearer: with COVID-19, it has become a case of being confronted to the same evil. A globalised evil. Epidemic, pandemic, panic, disarray. With the arrival of COVID-19, a common vocabulary takes shape: fear, death, shortage, mask, confinement.

The prevailing discourse presents the arrival of COVID-19 as a stark change. For our lives, in our societies. For Iran, it is quite the opposite. How can one speak of change, of novelty, of a new look in Iran, where death in fear is a daily affair? For most of the world, COVID-19 is an unprecedented event. A discovery. It is the same COVID, no doubt. But for the Iranians, it's a déjà vu situation. Here it is something new, but that something has always existed elsewhere. The gap is real.

When COVID-19 arrived, we had the impression that we were losing some of our freedoms, including the ban on gatherings. Demonstrations became forbidden. This freedom, suspended for a mere few weeks, is simply non-existent in Iran. No gatherings are tolerated there. And it is not because of COVID. The survival of the system is at stake. One example, shortly before the pandemic erupted:

In November 2019, a nationwide revolt is organised. Despite being banned from demonstrating, Iranians take to the streets. They denounce the inflation, which is at its historic height, they denounce the growing isolation of the country. Because the fascist regime exports its money, its men, its methods of oppression and assassination, to the Middle East, to Iraq, Syria, Lebanon, and, in exchange, it imports poverty, misery, embargoes for its people. The regime keeps defying the great powers of this world. And the people pay the price. When the same people took to the streets to say that they cannot stand it any longer, the anti-riot police opened fire without any restraint on the demonstrators.

While the people are being massacred, the regime dares to cut off the internet within the whole country, so that nothing circulates. Once again, so that what is happening does not get to be known. It is therefore quite disconcerting to note that the 'new measures' promulgated around the world to counter COVID-19, have in fact been in place in Iran for more than forty years. Here, temporary. There, institutionally. Only, these measures, imposed by force, are not there to protect or preserve human life. Far from it. They serve the interests of a fascist regime.

Here is another example of the chasm: social distancing. A new term for our unconscious. Our collective unconscious. But elsewhere, it has always existed. Social distancing is the basic rule in Iran. Men keep a distance from women. Do not shake hands with women. Do not touch. No physical contact. In more direct words, the distancing there is gender segregation. A formal interdiction to enjoy. This is not the only parallel. There are other equivalences. There, what need for a mask? There is the veil, the *chador*.

COVID-19 is also, unfortunately, counting the dead. Numbers are needed, statistics are established, a reliable discourse is constructed to evaluate the damage caused by COVID-19. In Iran, nothing is reliable. For example, death certificates are established in such a way as to hide the real reason for death: 'respiratory problem', or another disease is found in the deceased person. No telling of the truth, no mention of COVID-19. The statistics that are presented need to be appealing to the world. Untruth. Fake news. Abominable weapons to avoid losing face. Another state lie.

Now, let's dissect the management of COVID-19 by the Islamic Republic. It is edifying. First chapter, February 2020. The masquerade: the regime gives no information on the pandemic, and chooses to lie to its people. The annual show that is the anniversary of the Islamic revolution needs to be organised. And then, the rigged elections have to take place. Second chapter, March 2020. Paranoia and stupidity without measure. When he can no longer lie, when the whole world is confronted with the pandemic, the Supreme Leader speaks of a conspiracy organised by the Americans to weaken the regime, with the complicity of the 'jins'! Thirdly, as the health crisis takes a hold of Iran, as everywhere else in the world, the government could have decreed a lockdown. The government could have tried to preserve lives. Since only a few weeks before the arrival of COVID, its mercenaries, its basijis, its Revolutionary Guards and its anti-riot police were killing people in the streets. But caught at the throat with a collapsing economy and overwhelmed by the chain of events, the Supreme Leader asks the population to go to work. The wheels of the economy have to keep turning. COVID revealed the economic fragility everywhere. While the powerful economies invited or even forced their population to stay at home . . . the Islamic Republic, the regime that has no problem with death, that murders its population in cold blood, invites, incites citizens to go to work. To keep the economy running.

They sent people to work. In other words, the Iranians are sent to the slaughterhouse. In Iran, no one waited for COVID-19 to talk about catastrophe.

On 8 January 2020, in the early hours of the morning, a Ukrainian plane is shot down by Iranian missiles. Onboard this plane, among other passengers, were students and researchers living in Canada. According to Ukrainian forensic scientists, when the missiles shot down the plane, everyone was standing. Just for a moment, imagine the scene. You are in flight. Unfastened. Coming to understand what is happening. Saying to yourself: something is happening. You stand up, you try to do something, you look for a way out . . . and there is absolutely nothing that you can do. Utter helplessness. A total of 176 people perish – students, researchers, living people who weren't looking for death. They were going towards life. But the Islamic Republic decided to annihilate them.

This happened a few months ago. But my pain comes from even further away. Here we have been locked down and our governments have repatriated us from all corners of the world. But know that one can also be confined outside of one's home. There are those who were confined before their time. Exiles who never return. The displaced. The waste of lives.

I spell their names aloud.

I quote the name of Reza Baraheni, in exile and confined since 1998. Imagine a city. Toronto. Imagine its suburbs. Richmond Hill. Imagine far away. Even further. Imagine the distance that never ends. Those empty streets. Those houses that all look alike, that do not look like anything. Imagine a ghost town. I went there before COVID. I went there to see my friend Reza Baraheni. He opens the door, he doesn't recognise me. His memory has already fled. He lives here with his wife and children. He left Iran when the Ministry of Intelligence organised the 'serial' assassination of Iranian intellectuals and writers. I meet him several times. On the last day, he walks me to the door, points to a tree in front of his house, and says to me: 'Have you seen the secret agent hidden behind this tree'? His worried look is engraved in my memory.

I quote the name of Gholam-Hossein Sa'edi. A great writer. Forced to leave Iran after the 1978 Revolution. He settled in France. He was a doctor by training. But he chose destruction. He chose alcohol. To be torn away from one's country, one's language, and to find oneself here, in the unknown, faced with the unknown. He is one of those confined before his time had rung. Several photos show him, alone, hands above his head, locked up in his apartment.

In every country, every city, every cemetery, I come across people who are no longer there, who could not be repatriated. In Geneva, I don't know what kind of magic led me to the tomb of Mohammad-Ali Jamalzadeh. He is considered to be the founder of the Persian short story genre. In the first years of my life, when my childhood was being bombed by the war with Iraq, I lived in a street named after him. On his grave, a photograph. Sitting, staring at who knows where. A gaze like Nietzsche's, when he had stopped looking, when he had turned towards the impossible, towards a place unreachable.

I can also imagine Reza Baraheni in Toronto, sitting, looking at the impossible.

I now quote the name of Sadegh Hedayat. Under censorship, he was forced to go to India to publish his major work in the form of a manuscript. From one exile to another, he settled in France. And he notes, from afar, that everything is at risk of loss: it is impossible to publish freely in Iran, and it is equally impossible to stay away without suffering. It is impossible to witness the endless night that falls on your language, on your being, on your desires, on your impulses and to say nothing, to do nothing. Once, he throws himself into the river Marne. In the hope that his despair will come true. In vain. He goes elsewhere. Paris, eighteenth century. And as soon as he arrives, even before his new exile begins, he opens the gas in his room. He wants to end it for good. The presence of his inanimate body, lying on the floor, a thousand miles away from his language and from his work, signs this indisputable observation: there is nothing left to do. The Blind Owl, his main work, lives forever in our sleepless nights. I would like to quote an excerpt:

> There are wounds which, like leprosy, gnaw at the soul, slowly, in solitude. These are pains that cannot be opened up to anyone. Everybody considers them to be extraordinary accidents, and if anyone ever describes them in words or in writing, people, respectful of commonly accepted ideas, which they themselves share, try to welcome his story with an ironic smile. Because humankind has not yet found a cure for this scourge. The only effective medicines are the forgetfulness provided by wine and the artificial sleepiness provided by drugs or narcotics. The effects are, sadly, only temporary: far from calming down definitively, the suffering soon becomes exasperated again.

I can spell dozens and dozens of names of other lives wasted. I think of:

Mohammad Mokhtari and Mohammad-Ja'far Pouyandeh, intellectuals and writers, who died suffocated.

Ahmad Miralaï, translator, who was executed, his death due to an insulin injection that caused cardiac arrest.

Daryoush Forouhar and his wife Parvaneh Eskandari. Two political opponents, stabbed to death. Then Parvaneh Eskandari's breasts were cut off. The feminine again denied.

I quote the names of Karoubi and Moussavi, two reformist candidates facing Ahmadinejad in 2009. The elections were rigged. Ahmadinejad was re-elected, triggering the green movement in Iran. Hundreds of thousands of Iranians went out to protest in the streets. A few months later, after opening fire on the protesters, after the torture, the rape, the killing of the citizens who were protesting, they put Moussavi and Karoubi in confinement without trial. No way out. No contact with the outside world. They became prisoners in their homes. This home imprisonment has been ongoing for almost ten years. Some time ago, a picture of Moussavi and his wife, Rahnavard, was made public: they are unrecognisable. Utterly destroyed. Let's imagine, for a moment: ten years locked up at home.

It is clearly impossible to imagine the Iranian regime safeguarding the lives of its citizens. While COVID-19 was spreading, the risk of contamination was so high, it sometimes became impossible to bury loved ones. Again, in Iran, this is nothing new.

In the summer of 1988, just after the war between Iran and Iraq, Khomeini issued a fatwa. If the political prisoners did not repent, they would be executed. This brief. The sole purpose of this fatwa was to allow the executing of thousands of political prisoners. Almost 12,000 victims. Most of them buried in secret. In mass graves. It is said there are no political prisoners in Iran. The regime simply suffocates their existence.

Not being able to bury their loved ones. Suffocated to death. In Iran this has always existed. In every cemetery, where arrested lives are kept, in every city, in every country, there are people, there are names. There are graves. Not here.

One last example of COVID-19 in Iran. To try to show you how this evil I am talking about, which comes from far away, keeps going. There is a video, from March 2020. A group of men is seen from afar. The scene is being filmed from someone's mobile phone. The group, clearly panicked, starts running. As if they were being chased. This is probably the case. But nothing is seen behind them. As if some invisible force makes these men run away. Later, we learn from the media that they were a group of prisoners. They had been incarcerated in a prison in Iran, and had chosen that day to escape. They had probably heard about the arrival of COVID-19. And having neither recourse nor help, they had realised that they were being left behind. Abandoned. They had realised that their lives were worthless, and that their fate was of no importance to anyone. After experiencing isolation and loneliness within four walls, only COVID would come to get them; only COVID would come to meet them. So, instead of staying there to die, these prisoners escaped. Later, they are arrested. The story follows several versions from there. It is said that Iraqi Kurds arrested them and then handed them over to the Iranian authorities. The regime claims that it was the 'inhabitants' who arrested them. Among these prisoners is Shayan Saïdpour, charged a few years earlier for homicide, at the age of seventeen. As an example, in order to frighten the other prisoners, Shayan Saïdpour and some others in the group were executed. The message the regime sends is clear: either you stay in prison to die, or they will come to get you. But not to bring you back to life. To give you death.

I come back to my original question: Is it really possible to talk about COVID-19 in the same way everywhere in the world? In what context, under what regime does this virus arise? In Iran, COVID-19 came under a regime that denies life. A regime that is always on the side of death. That pushes its people into mass graves. That rapes its opponents in hidden prisons, kills those who dare contradict it, sends mercenaries to shoot intellectuals, writers, poets, in the four corners of the world.

Dégh kardan: it is a verb in Farsi. It is part of our everyday language. It means: to die of grief. Reza Baraheni once wrote a poem, addressed to a woman. Her name is Iraneh, Iran. He is confined to this house that will never be his home. And he confides in this woman. He tells her that he is going to die of grief, far from this woman, far from this country. To die of grief, then. *Dégh kardan*. It is the real disease, the virus of the invisible people. I would like to quote again Baraheni, and read an excerpt from his novel, forbidden since the time of the Shah.

> By cutting out his tongue, we forced him to endorse his own suffocation. We transformed his language into a memory in his brain and, as a result, we walled him up in the silent ruins of his memory. We taught him to contain our cruelty in his brain alone and to never be able to say a word about it again.

We have to talk about evil, or we will die of grief. Finally, a word from Edmond Jabès:

> Those from whom the right to live has been taken away, deserve, at least, a thought . . . a thought that would be their right.

(Translated from French by Chloé Pretesacque.)

BIBLIOGRAPHY

Castoriadis, Cornelius. *La fin de l'histoire*. Paris: Du Félin, 1992.
Latouche, Serge. *La planète des naufragés*. Paris: La découverte, 1991.
Rahnema, Majid. *Quand la misère chasse la pauvreté*. Paris: Fayard, 2003.
Traoré, Aminats. *Le viol de l'imaginaire*. Paris: Actes Sud, 2001.
Warin, François. Notes de cours et correspondances personelles.

14

'SHUFFERING AND SHMILING'

Life, Disease and Death in Burkina Faso

Aïdas Sanogo

This chapter looks into the discourses and practices of a few Ouagadougou dwellers (myself included) that went through different emotional stages during their city's lockdown due to COVID-19, from late March to early May 2020. I borrow the term 'shuffering and shmiling' from the artist Fela Anikulapo Kuti, who used it in his 1978 hit to refer both to the resilience of his fellows Nigerians and Africans in general, towards life's hardships. Facing hard times with an everlasting smile hanging on their face, indeed seems to be the daily script of millions of Africans, rehearsed over and over throughout their lifetimes. Author Maya Angelou also refers to the 'shuffering and shmiling' frame of mind in her spoken-word poem 'The Mask' to illustrate Black Americans' resilience throughout centuries.[1] One of my interlocutors aptly captured this mindset when he stated:

> As for us Africans, we always say we are ok even on the deathbed, you know? The day an African tells you 'I am not ok', my sister run! It means that he will pour the entire world's misery at your feet.[2]

Ouagadougou dwellers are not strangers to this constant hustler mindset. Like millions of urban dwellers in so-called Third World countries, they have to navigate through a whole package of thorny equations from sunrise to sunset: difficult access to running water, electricity provision issues, tricky (and sometimes deadly) road traffic, unemployment, underemployment, clientelism, inequity, impunity, various shades of structural violence, unfriendly weather, malaria, hunger. The COVID-19 pandemic was thus considered by many of those I interacted with, as yet another unknown brought to the multiple equations they had learned to live with against all odds.

Before digging into the ethnographic data, I briefly present a few COVID-19 and non-COVID-19 related data about Burkina Faso and the city of Ouagadougou, in particular.[3] Following this overview, the chapter is articulated around a vignette which narrates some of the encounters I had with seven Ouagadougou dwellers. Names have been changed for anonymity purposes. The exchanges were held in different languages (Jula, 'Burkinabè French' and French). They are translated in English throughout the text, though I do provide the original citations in endnotes, to remain as loyal as possible to my interlocutors' statements. The ethnography's time length (six weeks) could hardly be considered as sufficient to draw a relevant analysis from an anthropological perspective. I thus conclude with some general thoughts stemming from the vignette.

The very first COVID-19 cases in Burkina Faso were registered on 9 March 2020 in the capital city Ouagadougou. A religious leader and his wife who had come back from an international church meeting in Mulhouse (France) the previous month, both tested positive and officially declared as the 'Burkinabè patients zero'. On 11 March 2020 the World Health Organisation (WHO) declared that the COVID-19 epidemic had become a pandemic. On 14 March 2020 the Burkinabè government announced the closure of all educational establishments (kindergarten, primary, secondary, university and professional) from 16 March to 31 March 2020 throughout the national territory. On 18 March 2020, the first death caused by COVID-19 was registered. The deceased was a politician lady in her early 60s. On 22 March 2020 the Burkinabè government set in place a curfew from 7 pm to 4 am all over the country.

On 23 March 2020 exactly two weeks after the first case, there were officially 114 registered COVID-19 cases spread over four cities: Ouagadougou, Bobo Dioulasso, Houndé and Boromo. Many of those who tested positive were international travelers, government members, ambassadors, health agents, religious leaders as well as all those who were in direct contact with them: family, friends, colleagues and acquaintances. On 26 March, more than thirty markets were closed in Ouagadougou, to reduce the contagion risks. Social measures were implemented by the government to help the most affected business lines in urban areas: entertainment, transport, market, to name a few sectors. The said measures mostly consisted in allowances, food, tax reliefs, electricity and water bills payments. Following the social pressure applied by traders on the government, the main market of Ouagadougou (Rood-Woko) was reopened on 20 April 2020 despite the growing number of infected people in the country. On 27 April 2020, the Burkinabè government implemented the compulsory wearing of face masks all over the country. On 9 May 2020, two months after the first COVID-19 case was declared, there were officially 48 deaths due to the pandemic and 748 ongoing positive cases.[4]

To provide a better context and understanding of the coming vignette, it is important to look into non-COVID-19 related national data. On 8 March 2020, just a day before the first COVID-19 cases were officially declared in Burkina Faso, terrorist attacks killed forty-three civilians in two villages located in the Northern part of the country. About ten days prior to this attack, on 29 February 2020, ten police officers were killed in a terrorist attack targeting a police station in the city of Sebba, located in the Northern part of Burkina Faso. Another key data worth highlighting at the national level prior to COVID-19 breakout was the arm wrestling between the government and national unions. In February 2019, the Burkinabè government had stated that taxes on civil servants' allowances would be levied from February 2020 onwards.[5] Unions rejected the decision and had planned several protest marches for March 2020, which were later postponed due to the barrier measures implemented to reduce COVID-19 propagation. In the following lines, I describe how some Ouagadougou dwellers' discourses and practices fluctuated throughout the city's lockdown that lasted from 27 March to 4 May 2020.

I met Souleymane on the first Saturday of April 2020. It had been two weeks since I had been back from the city of Manga where I lecture, to stay with my family in Ouagadougou. I did my best to remain indoors and restricted myself from visiting anyone, my beloved grandma included. In retrospect, a part of me is convinced that I did so to protect her. The other part (the honest one) would admit that I was probably scared to death to step outside, after following COVID-19-related news on various media for three weeks in a row. I thus shamelessly stayed indoors thanks to the privilege that allowed me to do so. I eventually reached my limit and started to gradually take a step back from any news related to COVID-19. This alleviated my fear and allowed me to accompany my mother to a granite quarry, where she wanted to purchase some specific stones to improve her late father's grave. Together with her siblings, they had planned to commemorate a key anniversary of their father's death. They had modified their planned activities but eventually decided to complete the grave's construction which they had started before the COVID-19 outbreak in Burkina Faso. Both my mother and I were riding down the paranoia wave we had jumped on, a couple of weeks before. This resulted in us shifting what we considered 'an essential errand' in mid-March and what could pass as an 'essential errand' in early April. Armed with our face masks, we headed to the Pissy granite quarry after a ten-minute drive.

To anyone who has ever read Emile Zola's Germinal, I would not need to further describe this granite quarry. It was not my first time there so I knew what to expect: an open air field filled with granite (black, white and grey), darkened sand on which men, women, teenagers, children walk, run, ride and drive, from sunrise to sunset, in what could be termed as an orchestrated chaos. They all know their roles; they focus on it tirelessly in well-oiled movements: women of all ages break the granite blocks into small pieces (barehanded or with gloves on), some men carry the newly broken gravel on their heads, to gradually make piles of gravel that will eventually attract potential customers' eyes from afar. Other men (a bit younger than those who carry the gravel on their heads) frequently disappear and reappear in and from one of the mines further down, to bring back unbroken blocks of granite to the women. A few children play around bare feet or with shoes on, while teenagers follow the prescribed gender division of labour: girls break granite along with their grandmothers, mothers, sisters or friends and boys carry loads of gravel to the best of their capacities along with their fathers, brothers and friends. Some among the men in the granite quarry are (better) dressed while others are either shirtless or wearing tank tops soaked with perspiration. The (better) dressed ones are those who welcome customers like my mother, show them around; help them make their choices, negotiate prices between the women breaking the granite, the customer and the moto taxi driver that will carry the gravel from the quarry to its final destination once it is bought. There were also truck drivers among the male population: they would drive with the right dose of skillfulness and craziness in the narrow paths that wind through the quarry, to load bigger amounts of granite and/or gravel that the moto taxis cannot carry. The noise and smell emanating from the granite quarry are also something that one cannot easily forget. Indeed, the constant sound of rocks being hit and broken into small pieces, the honking of trucks, moto taxis, motorbikes, the joyful sound of children playing, sometimes interrupted by their unavoidable follow-up cries from time to time, the occasional booming noise coming from the earth's bowels, all this sprinkled by a linguistic variety which reflects the linguistic and cultural wealth that Burkina Faso possesses, like so many other countries around the world. The Pissy granite quarry is a small-scale mine, using an artisanal mining method to extract granite. To do so, men use old tires that constantly burn so that the heat will help split the granite. The permanent burning of tires gives a specific burnt plastic odor to the place, coupled to the dust cloud that is at times thick or thin but ever present.

It was not my first time to the granite quarry so I knew what to expect. I had known this quarry for more than fifteen years. Yet, I still felt self-conscious wandering there on 4 April 2020 wearing my face mask, while those surrounding me did not wear any mask, though their work environment exposed them to respiratory diseases way before the COVID-19 pandemic. Souleymane was among the (better) dressed men that played the broker role between customers and granite breakers. While he guided my mother through the quarry to help her make a choice, I slowed down and struck a conversation with Marie, a young woman in her late thirties, who tried to sell me some gravel. To my question why was she not wearing a mask, she smiled and answered that she could not breathe with a face mask.

> Some people can wear them, me I can't. It suffocates me. I heard that the ones sold at the pharmacy are a bit better but where will I find money to buy that? [. . .] With time you just get used it. How will we do? When you are busy looking for food, you don't think about anything else.[6]

When Marie realised that I would not buy her gravel, she lost interest in our conversation and resumed her granite breaking activity. I joined my mother and Souleymane about 300 meters ahead. They were closing up on the prices' negotiation. I asked Souleymane about the lack of face masks around us. He shook his head a bit, smiled and answered:

'Who has time for this? Corona is for those who have time, not us'.[7]

Intrigued by his statement, I asked him to elaborate. He first made sure to repeat instructions to the moto taxi driver who had agreed to carry the gravel my mother had just bought. When we were on our way back to the car, he came back to me:

'Corona is for White people and rich people, it is not here. They created this disease to kill their old people that's it. What is killing us here is blood pressure and diabetes'.[8]

To this, my mother asked him whether he was sure of his allegations. He replied with confidence:

> Madam it's true ooh! They lied when they said that people died of Corona here in Burkina, it is not true. White people, they want to get rid of their old people, that's it. [. . .] But if they kill all of them, who will they turn to for advice?[9]

The conversation continued till we reached the car and parted ways with Souleymane. The encounters with Marie and Souleymane represented a harsh reminder to me of how privileged I was, to be able to work from home and still get an income. I had heard and witnessed conversations from late March to early May 2020 about the causes of the pandemic, sometimes linking it to a curse sent from above to punish sinners. I had also heard several fellow Ouagadougou dwellers about the necessity to use prayer and fasting as a proactive way to fight the pandemic. However, the Pissy granite quarry workers used other lenses to react.

Like most Ouagadougou dwellers, Marie and Souleymane had their own ideas of what caused COVID-19 and how one might protect herself or himself against it. One of the striking differences in their approaches was that they did not apprehend the disease as a pandemic. Souleymane's words 'Corona is for White and rich people' noticeably show that he did not identify himself (nor all those working in the same conditions like him) as someone who could possibly be vulnerable to the disease. He had a clear geographical and social mapping of those affected by the disease. Both his social status and geographical location excluded and protected him from COVID-19. His understanding of the disease could be interpreted as if the Corona virus did not affect those who were at the bottom of Maslow's pyramid. If the disease was this selective, it could thus not be depicted as a pandemic and as such, he would rather worry over what directly concerned him – the hand to mouth occupation that ensured his survival – rather than try to find solutions for others who could not care less about him.

Marie had a slightly similar approach, though a bit more nuanced. Indeed, whether she acknowledged that COVID-19 was a pandemic or not, there was not much she could do about it. She could not afford to protect herself while making a living prior to COVID-19. She had had a couple of work accidents that obliged her children and her to spend weeks solely relying on their neighbours' solidarity, until she was able to fully resume work. Her logic was that she was more directly vulnerable to hunger and scarcity than she was to a potential exposure to a deadly disease. Shouldering the responsibility to 'put food on the table' for her children, required so much energy that she did not have much left to worry about the pandemic.

Both Marie's and Souleymane's stands mirrored the mindset of many Ouagadougou dwellers I encountered and to a certain extent, Burkinabè citizens residing outside the capital, irrespective of their social status. This could be linked to several reasons; I will however highlight two of them.

First, COVID-19 was brought into the country by intercontinental travelers. About half of Ouagadougou dwellers I interacted with over these six weeks had never been outside of Burkina Faso, let alone outside the continent. As one of them told me, 'I don't even own a passport and I am threatened by this thing, that's unfair'.[10] The Burkinabè government furthermore contributed (at least during the first month) to the idea that COVID-19 mostly affected affluent citizens, by refusing to communicate the identity of lambda citizens affected by the disease, to prevent any stigmatisation. Only public figures that tested positive were revealed: ministers, religious leaders, ambassadors and so on. This made it hard for the lambda citizens to identify with a disease that seemed to solely affect 'big people'.

Second, the country's internal turmoil at the social, political and economic levels prior to COVID-19 was equally reflected among Ouagadougou dwellers. Most of those I interacted with had directly or indirectly lost someone due to terrorist attacks during the past five years. The ongoing arm-wrestling between the unions and the government had also cast some shade on Ouagadougou dwellers' well-being. If anything, COVID-19 then simply added up to other pressing issues that had my interlocutors 'shuffering and shmiling', for lack of other alternatives, because 'life must go on against all odds'.

NOTES

1. https://www.facinghistory.org/resource-library/mask-maya-angelou. Last accessed 20 June 2020.
2. Ça seulement là, si c'est nous les Africains là, on dit toujours que ça va. Même si c'est chaud comment, comment, on dit ça va. Tu vois non ? Le jour où un Africain te dit 'ça va pas', walaye ma sœur faut courir ! Problème qu'il va décharger sur toi là, Dieu seul sait ! Informal discussion, M. O. 25 April 2020, Ouagadougou.
3. The data are drawn from personal notes written between 9 March 2020 and 10 May 2020. I also drew on the online newspaper www.lefaso.net
4. Source: https://lefaso.net/spip.php?article96754, last accessed 20 June 2020.
5. Source: https://lefaso.net/spip.php?article95121, last accessed 20 June 2020.
6. Dow bi sé ka don, né ti sé. Abada. N' gna mè ko pharmacie ta ka fusa doni, mais n'bo wari bo mi? [. . .] Doni doni, on est habitué. On va faire comment? Ni bi ka dara doumouni gninina, temps téyi ka miri ko wèrè la. Informal discussion, Marie. 4 April 2020, Ouagadougou.
7. Qui a son temps ici ? Corona c'est pour ceux qui ont temps, pas nous. Informal discussion, Souleymane. 4 April 2020, Ouagadougou.

8. Corona c'est pour les Blancs et les môgôs puissants, c'est pas ici. Ils ont créé maladie là pour tuer leurs vieux, c'est ça. Ce qui nous tue ici là, c'est tension et puis diabète. Informal discussion, Souleymane. 4 April 2020, Ouagadougou.

9. Madame c'est vrai ooh ! Quand ils ditsen que les gens sont morts ici là, c'est pas Corona, c'est pas vrai. Les Blancs là, ils veulent se débarrasser de leurs vieux là, c'est ça. [. . .] Mais si ils les tuent eux tous, où ils vont gagner conseil encore ? Informal discussion, Souleymane. 4 April 2020, Ouagadougou.

10. Je n'ai même pas passeport et puis ils viennent pour manger leur piment avec ma bouche, ça c'est pas la sorcellerie ? Informal discussion, Caroline. 7 May 2020, Ouagadougou.

Part IV

SIGHTING EVIL 102

15

THE PROXIMITY OF DEATH AND THE REMOTENESS OF TOTALITY

Ivana Perica

At the beginning of the lockdown, a friend wrote a short essay on the 'immediate and the insignificant', struggling with the fact that literary writing on anything else but the virus seemed to be not only insignificant (not responding to the most acute issue) but even insensitive or reckless. At that time, I wondered why I was, in contrast to my friend, under the spell of thinking only in terms of 'the immediate and the insignificant' and did not feel a similar need for distancing by means of fiction or theory. However, whereas it was of existential importance for my friend to carry on with writing, I simultaneously learned that 'if one is inside a historical break, one only perceives the immediate, precisely the break, precisely that something fundamental is happening. One is not yet in the analytical dimension'[1]. And today, with the 'overcoming of immediacy' being the 'philosophical question',[2] it is essential to discuss the pandemic with regard to the passage of time between the enforced measures that limited 'life as we knew it' and the desired return to the presumed 'normality'

Let me kick off by stating the obvious: namely, that by its categorisation as a 'crisis', the contemporary pandemic evokes previous crises. Simultaneously, due to the centrality of death, this crisis emerges as radically different. It forces us into experiencing death in – for many – an almost unprecedented and manifold way: at first, through daily reports on the death toll in countries throughout the world, we encounter death as a simple numeric value; simultaneously, we are continuously exposed to real or really possible, individual deaths affecting our fellow citizens, comrades, family members, and friends; finally, we are compelled to imagine death as a singular event in history, as the death of us all. Due to this interlacement with death, the coronavirus crisis seems to differ from the last global crisis, the GFC, which with its exuberant economic consequences caused numerous suicides but was nevertheless discursively shaped as an economic 'breach' – a breach that struck abruptly and effected a series of subsequent 'cuts' in terms of shortening state budgets and reinforcing the agenda of the so-called 'thin state'. By way of contrast, today even Emmanuel Macron, who emerged as one of the by-products of this state of economic exception, estimates that the issue we are dealing with is not a mere financial and geopolitical challenge but an anthropological one. Specifically, 'what is at stake is the trade-off between economic activity and death'.[3]

Although there are obvious 'interacting dynamics'[4] between these two crises, by now the coronavirus episode has been experienced as a kind of stimulus of historical proportions: it seems that in a future retrospect, the year 2020 will not be accounted for as a return of the past or as a flashback to economic crises of the former century. Precisely due to this incomparability and the un*account*ability of the coronavirus crisis, I contend that the received languages of political philosophy and political theory prove to be unfit for assessing the present. One cannot reach out for wordings such as 'crisis', 'the world', 'capitalism', 'neo-liberalism' or even the 'left' and 'right' for their common meanings without running the risk of squeezing the radically new experience into received scholarly and intellectual boxes and thus exerting epistemic injustice to what *is*.

Before COVID-19, we knew that the end of capitalism was unimaginable but the end of the world was not. We knew that species were dying at an unprecedented rate yet the actions to stop this were often limited to 'lifestyle activism'.[5] It was not before the new virus entered the human biome that 'we' became able to imagine the end of the species, *our* species, irrespective of differences in geographical location, political regime, state of development or lifestyle. Indeed, it is 'sad fact' but 'we need a catastrophe to make us able to rethink the very basic features of the society in which we live'.[6] Whereas the economic mechanism of the 2008 recession created by the unfathomable undercurrents of the financial system was opaque to most of us, the 2020 crisis is graspable by everyone. Furthermore, notwithstanding blatant differences in disease impacts in Italy and India, or Sweden and the United States, the 2020 death toll has yielded hitherto unprecedented global solidarity among people. Consider, for instance, observations such as the following: 'Never before has the role of civic society, and the importance of strong and resilient public health systems, been celebrated by so many from all segments of the political spectrum'.[7] This refers to those who stayed in their homes as well as those who facilitated everyday survival: delivery men and women, shop assistants, medical workers, and grocery producers. Furthermore, due to its unselective global impact, the coronavirus crisis serves as a mass experiment with unexpectedly positive short-term effects on nature. All that steers public discussions towards considering practical solutions towards changing the habits of traveling, vacationing, clothing, eating, working, etc.

All this transfers the debates onto a level that merges multiple sectors of interest (political, ecological, economic and psychological), which in effect employs the totality of social and natural relations. We know that totality as a philosophical and political concept is in contemporary critique more controversial than an elaborately disputed concept; nevertheless, it continues to reverberate criticism negatively, as an echo of the 'end-of-history' paradigm and the consubstantial dismissal of master narratives that seemingly unavoidably presage totalitarianism. On the occasion of another historical loss of totality, Georg Lukács warned that the insight into totality cannot be enforced by an act of will or faith but depends on the state of collective consciousness that is on its part reliant on the stage of development of social history. Consciousness, either truly or falsely, is necessarily 'part of the historical process of development of that uninterrupted transformation of social being'.[8] Accordingly, Lukács rejected the idea of general human consciousness that could exist independently of its location in historical time and geographical space. (And one of the reasons why I reach out for Lukács is that his early master theory of 'Obdachlosigkeit' in a way corresponds to the 'abandoned condition' as theorised by Nancy, and Dwivedi and Mohan.[9] Simultaneously, we know that, in many aspects, Lukács' critical standpoint was of a distinctive kind, embedded in decisively different political conditions than contemporary philosophy can provide for. In my opinion, with its activation of totality the coronavirus alters something about the relationship of politics and philosophy or, more precisely, about the political constitution of philosophy. I will get back to this later.) For our present discussion it is important that the social being as construed by Lukács 'occurs in uninterrupted interaction with nature (exchange of matter between society and nature)'.[10] This means that every kind of consciousness of nature – be it 'nature awareness', 'ecological consciousness' or one of the 'Anthropocene' – is socially and historically mediated.

In the essay 'Tailism and the Dialectic', Lukács articulates this in an exceptional way. *Tailism*, which deals with the intellectual attitude and social position of philosophers who are merely 'tailing' social developments, offers food for thought that is provoking not only for our discussion *about* the crisis but also for the way the constituents of this discussion (its subjects and objects) are philosophically constructed. With this essay, Lukács attacks the critiques of *History and Class Consciousness* for not realising the true character of the exchange between the human subject and nature. According to his critics, Lukács argues, there exists a rather unproblematic separation of the human individual as subject and nature as its object. Against such a 'speculative approach', Lukács goes on to argue that their theoretical 'subjectivism' is, in fact, a result of a historical process, that is to say, a product of society.[11][12] It is striking to what extent Lukács' revision of the inherited philosophical subject–object constellation resembles positions that were later theorised as the Anthropocene. Yet his standpoint also essentially differs from the Anthropocene theory. Besides the fact that the 'Anthropocene's implicit philosophy of history' suggests a 'grasp of modernity that is entirely ignorant of the complex historical processes at the heart of the capitalist world-ecology and its cultures', it also entails 'practical proposals that are apolitical and narrowly technological'.[13] By way of contrast, a Lukácsian would insist that not only is our reflection on nature enmeshed in the historical conditions of its emergence but that the very object of this reflection – the virus – is a result of human intervention. Namely, we are not dealing here with 'a virus from outer space', as Laurie Anderson sung about, but with a virus engendered in unmistakably social conditions (this irrespective of whether it came as a result of capitalist incursion into a previously uncolonised bio-system or allegedly from a scientific laboratory). As a product of society, the virus by the same token is produced by nature. In both cases, ultimately, it is indifferent towards humanity – or 'us'.

We ourselves are not indifferent. Even cynics such as Michel Houellebecq, who remarked, 'We will not wake up after the lockdown in a new world. It will be the same, just a bit worse',[14] display an unmistakable commitment to this world, a commitment that by way of an implicit 'it should be otherwise'[15] calls us to action. Just as we know that the experts have been warning against zoonotic pandemics for decades, we also know that the only way this plague can and should be countered is by means of action. For this, it is clear that we cannot simply re-employ the age-old 'subjectivism', according to which 'Society struggles with nature'.[16] A discovery of a vaccine that would immunise 'us' against 'nature' is only halfway satisfactory. Moreover, the struggle at stake requires above all social struggle, a struggle within 'humanity'. Therefore, one should cease using singular for what is plural, 'humanity' for 'society'.

Lukács was not the only one to claim that in moments such as the current one 'everything depends on consciousness, on the conscious will of the proletariat'.[17] Indeed, with the coronavirus, there has emerged an almost unprecedented level of social consciousness, feelings of compassion and acts of solidarity that are caused by fears of extinction unparalleled since World War II. As Jean-Luc Nancy observed, this virus in effect 'communises us'.[18] Yet this emergence of community is not necessarily of a political kind, and because the corona community is only *potentially* political it has to undergo a transformation from its constitution as lived reality on the one hand towards its activation in political terms proper on the other – similar to what was the case with Lukács' own analysis of class consciousness (from *an sich* towards *für sich*). At the moment, we find ourselves precisely at this watershed. Therefore, rather than being merely 'banal',[19] the critical standpoint we find ourselves in is capable of instigating change – both in terms of philosophy and beyond; under the condition, however, that the communising experience were furthered towards action.

As this urge to action is not of a speculative kind but is very immediate indeed, it renders outdated one pertinent train of thought in our liberal modernity – one that has typically been first and foremost in the amalgam of aesthetic and political thinking since the second half of the twentieth century – that is, the proxy idea of *as if*. Namely, it is by the device of this *as if* that art and the aesthetic are believed to act in place of organised politics (as its placeholder or 'a stand-in for an absent politics').[20] Accordingly, organised politics itself is, although 'theoretically necessary', believed to be 'practically impossible'.[21] Clearly, this *as if* cannot account for survival in times such as these. (This is applicable to all previous crises as well; however, in these crises the theoretical purveyors of the *as if* were not influenced by this truly non-discriminating 'threat of extinction' and could carry on their idea of the political as endorsed by philosophic and aesthetic 'radical passivity'.[22] Undoubtedly, today 'we find ourselves in a different historical moment' (Nowak 2020). What we are experiencing is a cancellation of the *as if* in both the modern and postmodern idea of politics, the cancellation of lifestyle, aesthetic and micro-political solutions to global ecological and social urgency in favor of global politics:

> unless we [. . .] understand that this world is the cobelonging equally of everyone in sharing the mysterious but absolute certainty of its persistence, *and create political concepts and new institutions*, this ship might become either too small or too large to set sail ever again.[23]

It is due to this urgency that the crisis is altering something about the inherited suspiciousness regarding human action, reason and the idea of goal-oriented, organised politics.

The proletariat today has many faces. Of course, we need to discuss the applicability of its somewhat monolithic modern shape to our contemporary stage of late-capitalist globalisation. The reason why Lukács' idea of the proletariat was politically viable in post-revolutionary Europe and does not seem to be so in the contemporary period of neoliberal globalisation is that it was consubstantial with what he self-ironically invoked as a 'mysterious "third place"', namely the Communist Party; today we find ourselves in absence of such 'historical demon[s]' but realise that political top–down decisions and global binding agreements are vital.[24] As it stands, if philosophy traditionally wavers when it comes to defining how one might move from theoretical insight into the necessity of both global and total shift towards practical politics, the proposals for changing the course of politics are already on the table.[25] Therefore, speaking in absence of the aforementioned 'third place', I dare not be presumptuous and claim that it is the task of philosophy to realise, let alone undertake this move; yet besides acknowledging the abandoned condition of the human, the least philosophy can do is to abandon the radical passivity as a device of political resistance.

According to Lukács, the proletariat as a political subject is not conscious by definition but is nevertheless 'necessarily tied to becoming conscious'. However, this consciousness, although enabled by the objective forces of the progress of history, does not enter the mind spontaneously; once objectively ignited, it 'must *become* conscious'. It 'must become effective in the heads of people, in order to be realized'. This difference between spontaneous consciousness and reflected, acquired consciousness correlates with the difference between the proletariat and communists. At the moment, we reside within this very difference, in a passage from the objective state of 'proletarian consciousness' towards a potential 'communist consciousness', the consciousness that prolongs the aforementioned event of communisation. In this respect, Lukács addressed '[f]orms of organization' which 'are there in order to bring this process into being, to accelerate it, in order to make such contents conscious in the working class (in a part of the working class)'.[26] The double valency of the proletariat – as a potentially conscious class and a truly conscious and organised class – is best displayed in times after the immediate peak of a crisis has been overcome. This is the moment where the petty *homo economicus*, after surviving the crisis by a whisker, usually resumes his or her exuberant buying, spending, investing – in sum, the private consumption of our common resources and gaining profit from them. The question that remains is about how to keep the *homo economicus* in detention while releasing only his/her/its conscious part (as if we all were composed of a Dr. Jekyll and a Mr. Hyde), that is, how to go on living under restraint.

NOTES

1. Hamza et al., 'An Interview with Karl-Heinz Dellwo'.
2. Lukács, 'Tailism and the Dialectic', 94.
3. Tooze, 'We are Living Through the First Economic Crisis of the Anthropocene'.
4. Antoniades, 'The Pandemic and the Day After'.
5. Sotirakopoulos, *The Rise of Lifestyle Activism.*
6. Žižek, 'Coronavirus is "Kill Bill"-Esque Blow to Capitalism'.
7. Neves and Merrill, 'Encouraging European Solidarity'.
8. Lukács, 'Tailism and the Dialectic', 103.
9. Nancy, 'Communovirus'; Dwivedi and Mohan, 'The Community of the Forsaken'.
10. Lukács, 'Tailism and the Dialectic', 103.
11. Lazslo Rudas and Abram Deborin.
12. Lukács, 'Tailism and the Dialectic', 98, 49.
13. Hartley, 'Anthropocene, Capitalocene, and the Problem of Culture', 155.
14. Houellebecq, qtd. in AFP, 'World Will Be Same but Worse'.
15. Adorno, 'Commitment', 194.
16. Lukács, 'Tailism and the Dialectic', 49.
17. Ibid., 56.
18. Nancy, 'Communovirus'.
19. Houellebecq, qtd. in AFP, 'World Will Be Same but Worse'.
20. Bernstein, *The Fate of Art*, 269.
21. Adamczak, *Beziehungsweise Revolution*, 84.
22. Wall, *Radical Passivity*; cf. Sotirakopoulos, *The Rise of Lifestyle Activism.*
23. Mohan, 'The Obscure Experience', my italics.
24. Lukács, 'Tailism and the Dialectic', 84.
25. Cf. Neves and Merrill, 'Encouraging European Solidarity'; Popic, 'Health Policy After The Crisis'.
26. All references in this paragraph to Lukács, 'Tailism and the Dialectic', 84.

WORKS CITED

Adamczak, Bini. 2017. *Beziehungsweise Revolution: 1917, 1968 und kommende.* Berlin: Suhrkamp.

Adorno, Theodor W. 1980 [1977]. 'Commitment'. In Ernst Bloch et al., *Aesthetics and Politics.* Translated by Rodney Livingstone, 177–95. New York and London: Verso.

AFP. 2020. 'World Will Be Same but Worse After "Banal" Virus, Says Houellebecq'. *France 24*, April 5, 2020. https://www.france24.com/en/20200504-world-will-be-same-but-worse-after-banal-virus-says-houellebecq.

Antoniades, Andreas. 2020. 'The Pandemic and the Day After'. *Social Europe*, May 15, 2020. https://www.socialeurope.eu/the-pandemic-and-the-day-after.
Bernstein, Jay M. 1993. *The Fate of Art: Aesthetic Alienation from Kant to Derrida and Adorno*. Cambridge: Polity Press.
Dwivedi, Divya, and Shaj Mohan. 2020. 'The Community of the Forsaken: A Response to Agamben and Nancy'. *European Journal of Psychoanalysis*, March 8, 2020. http://www.journal-psychoanalysis.eu/coronavirus-and-philosophers/.
Hamza, Agon, Frank Ruda, and Karl-Heinz Dellwo. 2018. 'An Interview with Karl-Heinz Dellwo: 68 – Aborted Liberation'. *Crisis & Critique* 5, no. 2: 354–75. http://crisiscritique.org/nov2018/dellwo.pdf.
Hartley, Daniel. 2016. 'Anthropocene, Capitalocene, and the Problem of Culture'. In Jason W. Moore, *Anthropocene or Capitalocene? Nature, History, and the Crisis of Capitalism*, 154–65. Oakland: PM Press.
Lukács, Georg. 2000. 'Tailism and the Dialectic'. In Georg Lukács, *A Defence of History and Class Consciousness. Tailism and the Dialectic*, 45–149. New York and London: Verso.
Mohan, Shaj. 2020. 'The Obscure Experience'. April 13, 2020. http://thephilosop hicalsalon.com/our-mysterious-being/.
Nancy, Jean-Luc. 2020. 'Communovirus'. Translated by Victoria Derrien. April 13, 2020. http://thephilosophicalsalon.com/our-mysterious-being/.
Neves, Catarina, and Roberto Merrill. 2020. 'Encouraging European solidarity: an unconditional basic income'. *Social Europe*, May 18, 2020. https://www.socialeurope.eu/encouraging-european-solidarity-an-unconditional-basic-income.
Nowak, Andrzej W. 2020. 'Philosophical Necromancy or Accelerationist Hope? A Response to Agamben'. *LeftEast*, April 13, 2020. http://www.criticatac.ro/lefteast/necromancy-or-hope-response-to-agamben/.
Popic, Tamara. 2020. 'Health Policy After The Crisis: More of the Same or a New Path?' *Social Europe*, May 18, 2020. https://www.socialeurope.eu/health-policy-after-the-crisis-more-of-the-same-or-a-new-path.
Sotirakopoulos, Nikos. 2016. *The Rise of Lifestyle Activism: From New Left to Occupy*. New York and Basingstoke: Palgrave.
Tooze, Adam. 2020. 'We are Living Through the First Economic Crisis of the Anthropocene'. *Guardian*, May 7, 2020. https://www.theguardian.com/books/2020/may/07/we-are-living-through-the-first-economic-crisis-of-the-anthropocene?fbclid=IwAR3OGSiqHfquCShx_O1D0Lq6l91XD_GFYtIissLpDncNWCmUOMySLhJatNU.
Wall, Thomas Carl. 1999. *Radical Passivity: Lévinas, Blanchot, and Agamben*. New York: Suny Press.
Žižek, Slavoj. 2020. 'Coronavirus is "Kill Bill"-Esque Blow to Capitalism and Could Lead to Reinvention of Communism'. *Ikaro*, March 19, 2020. http://www.revistaikaro.com/slavoj-zizek-coronavirus-is-kill-bill-esque-blow-to-capitalism-and-could-lead-to-reinvention-of-communism/.

16

'BUT (LET'S) DELIVER US FROM EVIL'

From 'Pandemic' Evil to Evil as 'Pandemisation'

Benedetta Todaro

On 11 March 2020 the World Health Organisation (WHO) stated, 'deeply concerned both by the alarming levels of spread and severity, and by the alarming levels of inaction, [. . .] have made the assessment that COVID-19 can be characterized as a pandemic'.[1] This term, 'pandemic', had already been used by the WHO in relation to influenza A (H1N1) in 2009 (commonly referred to as 'swine flu'), whereas in relation to severe acute respiratory syndrome (SARS) (commonly referred to as 'avian flu') in 2003 the WHO had used the term 'outbreak'[2] instead. What criterion legitimised this differential choice of terminology? If WHO's concerns about 'avian influenza' had focused primarily on a very high 'mortality rate', in the case of 'swine influenza' and COVID-19 instead there would have been concerns about the level of spread of the disease – that is, the contagiousness of the transmissible disease – that means that, from an epidemiological point of view, the 'attack rate' of the virus (also called the 'morbidity rate') becomes more significant than its 'mortality rate' (also called the 'virulence of the strain'). In other words, what seems to allow the use of the term 'pandemic' is the estimation of the *contagion power* (transmission power) of the virus and, therefore, of its *power of geographical expansion*. This observation seems to us quite banal today, in the midst of a global coronavirus crisis, and one might legitimately wonder whether this observation is not, in fact, already inscribed in the etymological difference between the terms 'pandemic' and 'epidemic'.

What, on the contrary, seems to appear as less banal is that, although it appeared for the first time in 1792 in the *Dictionnaire* by Trévoux, the use of the term 'pandemic' was, until the twentieth century, extremely rare. Indeed, the use of this word seems to us to be closely linked to the history of the birth of the WHO in that, since its foundation in the post-war period in 1948, it has consistently warned its member states that 'after experiencing three influenza pandemics in the twentieth century, there is no reason not to fear a new emergence of an influenza virus strain with pandemic potential in the twenty-first century'.[3] It would therefore be legitimate to ask whether the conditions of possibility for the creation of a *world* health organisation are not, essentially, the same conditions of possibility that allow a virus to manifest itself, so to speak, 'pandemically'. Indeed, would it be possible for a non-world organisation to warn the whole world about the possibility of a potentially 'global' evil? In other words, could we speak of 'pandemic' in a '*non-globalszed*' world?

Some would argue that pandemics have always existed and that the contagiousness of a disease is an intrinsic factor to it. However, it is sufficient to observe the statistical formula of *pandemic risk* to realise that the contagiousness of a disease, its transmissibility, depends only on one factor in three of the disease itself. Indeed, the so-called 'basic reproduction rate', on the basis of which the 'attack rate' is calculated, is the product of three elements: $R_0 = ßcD$. The factor

> ß refers to the probability per unit of time that a contagious subject transmits the virus to a susceptible subject with whom he is in contact, c the number of 'effective' contacts characterizing the inverse of the 'social distance' between the infectious and susceptible, and D the duration of the contagious period.[4]

We can say that, if factor D corresponds to the lifetime of the contagious nature of the virus, the first two factors (ß and c) are similar to nothing other than the *space-time coordinates* of our level of *global inter-connectedness*.

However, if 'the pandemic will be declared when $R0 > 1$'[5] and if, strictly speaking, we cannot act on the lifespan of the contagious nature of the virus, we can deduce that the risk of a pandemic is only real in a *globally interconnected world*. Thus, for the word 'pandemic' to find its field of operation, it is therefore necessary that the 'confines of the world' be attainable and this, in a short time delay. Indeed, the use of the term 'pandemic' seems to be justified exclusively by the fact that it has been shown that the dissemination of 'evil' can occur quickly, even *instantaneously*, and over a very vast space, even over the *entire globe*. Time *reduced to a minimum* (i.e. to the instant) and space *enlarged to a maximum* (i.e. to the globe), humanity could only have entered the 'age of pandemics' through a movement of *spatio-temporal totalisation* (or, we could say, 'pandemisation') of existence.

Without dwelling too much on this point, we would nevertheless like to suggest that if the word 'totality' and its harmful implications are, no doubt with good reason, easily traced back to the birth of the 'totalitarian states' of the twentieth century, state totalitarianisms are not the only representatives of this tendency to totalising systematisation which characterises that epoch, the twentieth century, as well as this one, ours, the twenty-first century. Indeed, we cannot fail to observe that while the 'totalitarian States' imposed, let us say, 'from the outside', although *on the body*, their totalising power, another power, much more sneaky and much less grandiloquent than that exercised by these States, was lurking in the shadows and was thus infiltrating *in the body*. We are referring here to the penetration *into* and *through* the *biologic-organic body*, that is, the body understood as an 'organism', of this trend in knowledge that has been developing since the 1920s and which is called 'general systems theory'. According to the definition of its 'initiator' Ludvig von Bertalanffy, 'general system theory, therefore, is a general science of "wholeness" which up till now was considered a vague, hazy, and semi-metaphysical concept'.[6]

Thus if the conditions of possibility of this 'pandemic evil', this 'global', 'total', 'organic', 'systemic' evil, are summed up, essentially, at the very fact of the possibility of a *totalising totality* – in its economic-march and actualisations, but also organico-systemic or even cybernetic – shouldn't we, instead of dealing with the repetitive task of treating the infection, think about eradicating our *infectivity*? Instead of launching, as the WHO advises, every thirty years or so, a desperate race in search of a salvific immunity principle, an anti-*this*-or-*that*-virus vaccine, should we not, rather, think of a *anti-pan, anti-global, anti-total, anti-organic immunity*, a kind of 'vaccine', not only 'anti-pandemic', but 'anti-pandemisation'?

In a world where pathology is, from now on, *pa(n)thology*, can we still hope in the benevolent action of the God – the Good, the vaccine, the *WHO* – ready to deliver us from his inseparable enemy, the Evil? In other words, if today Evil is *Pan*, can we still turn towards some providential Go(o)d? It would seem that we can no longer rely on ancient saving oppositions, one polarity of which would still be already preserved as if vaccinated against Evil, but that we must instead think of another kind of salvation, *anti-panic*, able to exorcise *this* Evil – the *total* Evil.

At least two options are opened to us.

The first one, the one currently being adopted around the world, is based on a world vision imbued with a Good–Evil bipolarism, with the inevitable equations (1) Evil = the Other, destroyer of the world, and (2) Good = the Self, saving sovereignty of the world. Thus this option combines *return* and *withdrawal* in a way: return to old ways of living, withdrawal into the comfortable and protective boundaries of the self. *Return to oneself and withdrawal within oneself.* Eulogy, therefore, of the return/withdrawal *to* and *in* the world of Newton and Descartes: *to* and *in* a 'closed system' (as opposed to the 'open system' of the *organic body*), to and in the 'mechanistic world' (as opposed to the 'dynamic', 'energetic' world of the *quantum*). These are all these local or national attempts at *sovereign entrenchment*: 'I barricade myself in my own home, and so much the worse for others' – affirmation of *exclusive ownership* of the Good, under the cover, moreover, of fine intentions tinged with *ecologism*, thus justifying the withdrawal by the will to 'save the world' (by the way, the other name for 'systemic thought' is, as Fritjof Capra reminds us, 'holistic' or '*ecological*'[7] vision of the world). This option, that of the demonisation of the Other and of the rescue of the Self, will, at best, soothe the *panic* feeling, without achieving the destitution of the reign of the 'pan'. Confronting *panikos*, that is the collective fear of the 'without object' – namely: the virus – only isolation, lockdown, avoidance, autarky, quarantine seem to be able to save us. This is an illusion with harmful consequences: to relieve ourselves of Evil instead of to free ourselves from it – *resistance* and not *revolution*.

The second option, on the other hand, is based on a completely different equation: Evil = totality. The totality of the world market, the totality of the organic body, the totality of the computer network etc.: everything seems '*to make system*' today, fertile ground for *virality*. '*To make system*', that is, not the *common co-existence* of all the existing people in the world, but *the generic interchangeability* of all the individuals in the world. What counts in a system, whether it is physical, economic, informatics or any other kind, are not its elements but, rather, their interconnections. Thus, the virus, the pa(n)thogenous agent of the system, kills 'anyone', in the sense of 'no matter who': we were sadly aware of this when the city of Bergamo, in Italy, transmitted to the world the images of funeral processions of military trucks transporting, to crematoria in other regions, elsewhere, the bodies that had succumbed to the virus. But elsewhere where? And whose body are they? Will they come back? Will they still be 'bodies'? Will they return to us only as 'bodies'? The only certainty we have is that they will be immediately *replaced* in intensive care.

That being said, if the solution of a *return/return* to what Shaj Mohan humorously but judiciously called 'idyllic a priori'[8] can hardly satisfy us, it would be necessary, through a gesture borrowed from Jean-Luc Nancy, to follow the auto-deconstructive movement of the 'making system' itself, and thus to assert, in the manner of Marx, its 'historical performance.'[9]

Thus we will see that the 'exact reverse'[10] of the totality of the system is not isolation, lockdown, avoidance, autarky, quarantine but what we have decided to call 'common immunity', which obviously has nothing to do with the far-fetched proposal of 'gregarious immunity', which, in order to function, must be based on the fact that part of the population is already immunised or even vaccinated. We know very well which part of the population, today, would benefit *in advance* and *for advance* from this kind of bourgeois mechanism of immunisation – as François Bégaudeau so aptly said, 'the privileged did not wait for the coronavirus to practice social distancing.'[11] But if, as Bégaudeau still affirms, a privileged is 'someone who does not undergo, or undergoes just a little, the physical world [because] the height of un individual's place on the scale of privileges is inversely proportional to the number of time per day when the physical world imposes itself on him'.[12] However, since the totality of the system has been pushed to its limits, that is to say that there is no longer the possibility for anyone, even temporarily, to escape it, today 'sudden reality imposes itself', *to all – without exception*. 'The actual virus', writes Bégaudeau, 'is mostly affecting poor people, but it has the ecumenical goodness to affect or even infect a few rich people'.[13]

Suddenly, the 'making system', having reached the end of itself, *reverses et revolts itself* in 'making world', in the common perception of our inevitable *being-in-the-world-with-others*.

NOTES

1. See 'Coronavirus Disease 2019 (COVID-19). Situation Report—51'.
2. World Health Organisation (2017), *Communicating Risk in Public Health Emergencies*, p. ix.
3. Flahault, 'Épidémiologie des pandémies grippales' my translation. In fact, in a document dated 2012, the *WHO* states that the member states: 'note the continuing risk of an influenza pandemic with potentially devastating health, economic and social impacts, particularly for developing countries which suffer a higher disease burden and are more vulnerable', 'acknowledge with serious concern that current global influenza vaccine production capacity remains insufficient to meet anticipated need in a pandemic' and, finally, 'acknowledge with serious concern that the distribution of influenza vaccine manufacturing facilities is inadequate particularly in developing countries and that some Member States can neither develop, produce, afford nor access the vaccines and other benefits': World Health Organisation (2011), *Pandemic Influenza Preparedness: Sharing of Influenza Viruses and Access to Vaccines and Other Benefits*, pp. 6–7.

4. *Ibid*, p. 493, my translation.
5. *Ibid*, p. 493, my translation.
6. Von Bertalanffy, *General System Theory,* New York: George Braziller, 1968, p. 37.
7. Capra, *La toile de la vie*, 20, my translation and emphasis.
8. Mohan, 'La Corona della Stasis', my translation.
9. Nancy, *The Creation of the World or the Globalization*, 36.
10. *Ibid*, p. 40.
11. Begaudeau, 'Le privilégié n'a pas attendu le coronavirus pour pratiquer la distanciation sociale', my translation.
12. *Ibid.*
13. *Ibid.*

BIBLIOGRAPHY

Begaudeau, François. 'Le privilégié n'a pas attendu le coronavirus pour pratiquer la distanciation sociale', *Socialter*, 4 March. http://www.socialter.fr/fr/module/99999672/887/le_privilgi_na_pas_attendu_le_coronavirus_pour_pratiquer_la_distanciation_sociale.

Capra, Fritjof. *La toile de la vie. Une nouvelle interprétation scientifique des système vivants*. Monaco: Éditions du Rocher, 2003.

Flahault, Antoine. 'Épidémiologie des pandémies grippales', *Revue des maladies respiratoires* 25 (2008): 492–496.

Mohan, Shaj. 'La Corona della Stasis', *Antinomie. Scritture ed immagini*, 9 May 2020. https://antinomie.it/index.php/2020/05/09/la-corona-della-stasis/.

Nancy, Jean-Luc. *The Creation of the World or the Globalization*. Translated by François Raffoul and David Pettigrew. Albany: State University Press of New York, 2007.

Von Bertalanffy, Ludwig. *General System Theory*. New York: George Braziller, 1968.

World Health Organisation. *Communicating Risk in Public Health Emergencies: A WHO Guideline for Emergency Risk Communication (ERC) Policy and Practice*. 2017. https://apps.who.int/iris/bitstream/handle/10665/259807/9789241550208-eng.pdf;jsessionid=14D32F8AD4BC3591E4A7952F07102BC0?sequence=2.

World Health Organization. 'Coronavirus Disease 2019 (COVID-19). Situation Report—51'. https://www.who.int/docs/default-source/coronaviruse/situation-reports/20200311-sitrep-51-covid-19.pdf?sfvrsn=1ba62e57_10.

17

NATURE'S REVENGE?

On the Coronavirus and 'Natural Evil'

Daniel J. Smith

Whenever one is faced with what looks like an unprecedented new problem for thinking, it is always a valuable exercise to return to the history of philosophy. But one should not do so in search of ready-made answers waiting to be transplanted into the present, as if Marcus Aurelius's meditations on the Antonine plague might secretly contain the solution to *our* plague. To ask a question like 'what would Seneca do?' is to indulge in a triviality worthy of a fridge magnet or a bumper sticker – it is not a serious philosophical question. These texts may be worth revisiting for other reasons, but philosophy long ago moved beyond its conception of itself as the search for timeless wisdom in the great books of the tradition, a shift that Deleuze summed up beautifully in his formula that 'there is no heaven for concepts'.[1] To really understand a text from the past one must grasp it *as* past, which means not only exploring the ways in which it resonates with contemporary experience, but also the ways in which it *no longer* speaks to us. Any unbridgeable gap marks the trace of a rupture in the history of thinking which the historically minded philosopher must try to explain. We could say the real object of the philosophical historian of philosophy is this very play of comprehensibility and incomprehensibility through which a certain vision of the past emerges from an implicit account of the philosophical present. Which concepts still make sense to us and which do not any longer? Are we witnessing the repetition of a debate that has already been had in another context and if so, what are the main differences, and how significant are they? Have the fundamental *problems* persisted, or have they gone through changes that should transform the whole horizon of questioning? This slow, patient kind of work does not promise immediate solutions to our undoubtedly pressing problems, but it can help in orienting ourselves, in taking a step back from the urgency of the crisis to take stock of the situation in terms of the long history of thought.

Considering our question – 'is it possible to talk of evil in the time of the pandemic?' – one should begin by saying that through most of the history of philosophy, 'evil' would have been the very first concept used to define a crisis like this one. Plagues, pandemics and other monstrosities were grouped together with phenomena like floods, earthquakes and hurricanes under the heading of 'natural evil'. This classification already cries out for interpretation in today's context since it's not obvious to us that these things should go together. Does a virus really belong in the same category as a hurricane? Surely not, but we do have a sense that this pandemic is in some way related to the climate emergency and so at least indirectly to other 'natural disasters', even if there is still some debate about the best way to characterize that relationship. The concept of 'natural evil' played a vital role in the history of metaphysics: if God is good, and if Nature bears the perfection characteristic of all his works, then how are we to explain the apparently senseless suffering caused by something like the novel coronavirus, which seems not to contribute to any 'higher' order but only to destroy everything it touches, for no purpose other than its own dead repetition of itself? It is worth remembering that this 'natural evil' posed a much more significant challenge to modern philosophy than the more familiar 'moral evil' of humankind. It is easy enough to blame moral evil on the misdeeds of freely acting human beings; far harder to do so for an earthquake or a pandemic. Unlike today, where 'evil' is a concept largely at the margins of contemporary thought, through much of the history of philosophy it was absolutely fundamental.

It is clear, then, that there has been a rupture in thinking since the modern period. If we feel able to speak of 'evil' at all today – and even this is not certain – it is generally at the register of 'moral evil'. Some actions are so heinous that no other word seems to capture the full extent of their hideousness, such as the man who allegedly spat on rail worker Belly Mujinga at Victoria Station in London, knowingly infecting her with the coronavirus that would take her life a few weeks later.[2] Similarly, we seem to have little trouble branding as 'evil' individuals in positions of power and authority when they seem to be prioritising their personal fortunes over public health (the reader can supply their own examples here – there are sadly many to choose from). But we would hesitate to label the virus *itself* 'evil' as the moderns would, even if we retain an obscure sense that there is some relationship between these terms – my grandmother calls it 'the evil virus', and I am sure she is not the only one.

How should we characterize this break? One popular answer would refer us to the waning of religion, and to the hypothesis of a 'death of God'. There are many reasons why I do not find this story convincing, but I will focus here on just one: it locates the shift too late in history. The specific rupture I am trying to describe arose *earlier* than the great confrontation between religion and atheism that characterizes nineteenth-century European philosophy in figures such as Feuerbach, Nietzsche, Marx and Kierkegaard. One can find the main elements of the break already in Kant, for whom atheism is still more or less inconceivable as a considered philosophical position.[3] So if it is not a question of religion pitted against atheism, then what does characterise this transition? I will define it by the following two points.

The first concerns *legitimacy*. The so-called 'problem of evil' is most fundamentally a question of legitimacy, in which the mere existence of evil poses a threat to order, divine or otherwise. Here philosophy shamefully puts itself in service of the existing powers, and takes up the task of minimizing, explaining away and justifying evil. I've long found it striking that through the history of Western philosophy, evil overwhelmingly shows up as a 'problem' in need of a solution and only rarely as a phenomenon to be grasped in its own right. When faced with something so extreme that it can only be described as 'evil', the first impulse of the philosopher when they come on the scene is to apologise for power by justifying the arrangement of the world that produced it in the first place. It is this justificatory impulse, first of all, that contemporary philosophy is no longer prepared to accept. One could invoke many names here, but I will just mention Levinas, who argued that the twentieth century marked the 'end of theodicy', not only in the sense that its numerous atrocities made those arguments finally unconvincing, but more profoundly that it revealed, in a general way, 'the outrage it would be for me to justify my neighbor's suffering'.[4] The most significant problem with theodicy is not that it makes theological assumptions or metaphysical errors but that it is *ethically* suspicious, an attempt to legitimate and justify that which ought to remain fundamentally illegitimate and unjustifiable.

Second, since the modern period, there has been a profound transformation in the concept of nature. From nature understood as a perfect expression of God's goodness to nature as fundamentally indifferent to our fates. From nature as the original source of all value, such that to be 'natural' is *eo ipso* to be 'good', to nature as that which is outside all value – 'before' good and evil, rather than beyond it. More recently, nature has also been re-thought in its relationship with many concepts to which it was traditionally opposed. For example, the very idea of a 'natural disaster' falls under suspicion today because human impact on the climate has been so profound that one cannot subtract a measurable human contribution from how nature would have acted had it been left to its own devices. For any given natural event, one can no longer say for sure that humans had nothing to do with it; one could say that *nature itself* has become 'man-made'. This certainly holds for the current pandemic: the bats and pangolins apparently responsible for infecting the unfortunate patient zero would likely never have come into contact with humans were it not for the hyper-exploitative labour conditions imposed by global agribusiness. A similar suspicion lingers over the other terms to which nature is typically opposed: we no longer readily accept distinctions between nature and civilization, nature and nurture, nature and culture and so on.

This brief historical excursus has revealed that philosophy *has* addressed this problem of the relationship between evil and pandemics before, but that it did so on the other side of a break. What does this mean for the question we are addressing today? It seems to me that this historical account, if we accept it, sets us two philosophical tasks. First, if we are truly confident in our judgement that this whole way of thinking must be abandoned, then that already implies a certain critical programme: to criticize any resurgence of the discourse of theodicy in the present and to identify any new variants of its logic that may have arisen within other discourses. Alongside the old *theological* problem of evil, there also exists what I call the *political* problem of evil: how does one reconcile a belief in the goodness of a particular political system with the existence of evil *inside* that system? The mere fact of poverty, hunger, or homelessness within the walls of the *polis* poses a radical challenge to the legitimacy of its rulers that is formally analogous to the one that the 'natural evil' of an earthquake once posed to the supposed sovereignty and goodness of God. When a state stands accused of some crime, its defence will usually follow the same argumentative pathways that were forged by Leibniz, Malebranche and other classical philosophers. It will be said that all poverty is certainly regrettable and sad, but that it is nonetheless justified because some level of poverty would exist even within the perfect state in the best of all possible worlds; that hunger arises not from any general will of the government, which must always be assumed to be good, but from particular circumstances that are beyond its reach and for which it cannot be held responsible; that homelessness arises not from a particular social order that is actively maintained and continuously re-created by the state, but from the free will of individuals who make bad choices.

And it is not only in politics that one finds mutations of this logic. It is especially prominent in economics, where no amount of destruction is too great to be pinned on the mysterious movements of an inhuman 'market' that is nevertheless still assumed to be essentially good. Its continued rule over us is typically justified through principles of development and growth that are supposed to be of a higher order than any negative effects it may have on those of us down below who suffer the consequences. The devastation it so often leaves in its wake does not constitute an argument against it, since its perpetual motion is thought to be the highest good, when all is said and done. One can encounter another mutation of the theodicy logic in some ecological thinking, where predicates traditionally attached to God are transferred to a reified 'Nature'. Pope Francis has called the current pandemic 'nature's revenge' against human beings for our various sins against it, from deforestation to mass extinction and climate systems breakdown. This is not a theodicy, a justification of God, but what could be called a *physiodicy*, a justification of nature understood on the model of sovereignty. So, the thesis of a historical break characterised by these two points demonstrates the need for a particular diagnostic task; a policy of philosophical track-and-trace, if you will, whereby new strains of theodicy are identified, quarantined and taken out of general circulation.

The second task is to think about whether there are other possibilities for a new and different deployment of this conceptual apparatus today. I don't have the space to develop a full-blown theory of evil in this short text, so I will just make some brief remarks about the relationship between the concepts of evil and nature. Does this overcoming of the old problem of evil mean that there is nothing more to say about nature? Is philosophy now essentially limited to making moralised statements of praise or condemnation of the things that our governments do in response to the virus? In spite of its name, the coronavirus does not care for sovereignty and it does not respect the borders we try to impose upon it, whether those are the geographical borders of our nation-states or the borders of the concepts with which we try to capture it. This suggests that we should leave space for nature understood in another of the ways it has been classically conceived, not as that which is essentially good, but as that which exceeds and indeed overwhelms any conception we may have of it – its sublimity. In this time of pandemic when so much is still unknown, we are witnessing that face of nature which goes beyond all sovereignty and which does not respond to our speech acts, much to the chagrin of demagogues like Trump, Bolsonaro, and Modi, whose usual political playbooks left them helpless in the face of the viral threat. The virus is not like a traditional enemy who wants to kill us and against whom we must defend ourselves; what is in a sense even more frightening is its *indifference* to our life or death. This is one of many reasons why the metaphor of a 'war' against the virus is so misleading – a war is something that happens between two entities that in some ways resemble one another; it is not a war in any meaningful sense if one's enemy operates at a completely different level.

I'd like to close these reflections by introducing a historical philosopher who puts forward a very different conception of 'evil' that I believe offers some interesting lessons in our time of pandemic. In the 1809 *Freiheitsschrift*, Schelling developed a highly original concept of evil through an analogy with *disease*.[5] The distinction between bacterial and viral infections was not introduced until 1892, some decades later, so it would not be too much of a stretch to say that for Schelling, a virus like this one provides precisely *the* figure for evil as such – a 'virality of evil', indeed. Where classical metaphysics says in various ways that evil does not exist, characterizing it in terms of privation, lack or non-being, Schelling insists that we must think it on its own terms as something with a reality all of its own. Disease gives him a model of something that is undoubtedly positive and real, but which retains the sense that something is out of place, that things are not as they should be. A disease occurs, on his account, when one part of an organism *usurps the place of the universal*, dominating the totality of its existence by arrogating the forces of the whole to itself. An eye infection, to use his example, does not affect only the vision because the organism reacts to it by inducing a fever that affects the body's capacity to do anything at all. There is no such thing as a localized disease of the part; disease is always a disease of the whole. Or think of the coronavirus: by attacking our lungs, it affects our behaviour by making us do specific things that help its transmission like coughing and sneezing. If it were instead to attack the kidneys, say, or the heart, that would not change the way we act in a way that spreads it further, instead killing us and itself in the process (it's well known that the relatively low death rate is the main reason the coronavirus has killed so many people). The centre is usurped and all the forces the organism can muster are directed to its new goal of propagating its unwanted visitor, whatever the cost to itself.

This analogy with disease, and especially with viruses, seems to me very effective at capturing certain forms of what we might still want to call 'evil' which are not grasped well by other popular accounts such as 'banality', the 'diabolical' or what Simona Forti has nicely termed the 'Dostoyevsky paradigm' of a powerless innocent victim facing off with an omnipotent evil perpetrator.[6] How can we understand the actions of those who have recently been driving vehicles into crowds of protesters, other than to say that their very existence has been hijacked by an ideological virus that has killed off all concern for anything other than its own spread? Or, one could think of politician Dan Patrick who infamously went on Fox news near the beginning of the first lockdown to argue that older people should be *willing to die* if that's what it would take to keep American malls open. He, too, is in the grip of a political virus, one that has so taken over his values that even the life-preserving *conatus* is sacrificed to the imperative that capital must continue to circulate. What's more, commentators have found themselves unable to resist metaphors of viruses and viral growth to explain the explosive spread of the new political nationalisms that have been sweeping the globe in recent years, from Britain to Brazil, from India to Israel. The virus of this far-right politics usurps even the self-interest of its hosts, generating a gleeful form of insatiable hatred that eventually destroys its subject as well as its object.

Finally, this account of evil as taking 'viral' form allows us to understand a curious phenomenon I mentioned earlier, namely our obscure sense that there is something evil about *the virus itself*. Of course, one could not seriously make such a claim in the contemporary context; to do so would be to return to the old conception of 'natural evil' that I've been arguing belongs on the other side of a fundamental rupture. However, there are some curious passages where Schelling speaks of 'preformed moral relationships' that exist already within nature, prior to any level where one would be able to speak of good and evil in the strict sense. What might this mean? Most fundamentally, a virus is the expression of a certain structure, a certain form, that actually exists at many different registers, characterised, as I said, by a hijacking of the organism's seat of universality. A virus is a lower expression of the very same process that is *evil itself* where it exists at the human level. The conspiracy theory that justifies the murder of innocents to the credulous troll harbouring fantasies of violence, I am suggesting, is formally analogous to an infectious disease, and is best understood in those terms. Even though it would be absurd and anachronistic to describe viruses as 'evil' in themselves, we nonetheless feel a kind of 'horror' towards them; Schelling explains that this is a genuinely *moral* feeling that is actually a perfectly rational reaction to a real prefiguration of evil in nature. We recognize the similarity to genuine spiritual evil – we see that if some *human* phenomenon were to take this form it would indeed be evil in the full sense – and it is this that provokes our disgust. Perhaps my grandmother is speaking some sense, after all, when she speaks of the 'evil virus'.

NOTES

1. Deleuze, *What is Philosophy?*, 5.
2. As reported in Madeley, 'There Are Devils Walking among Us'.
3. See Kant's essay 'On the Miscarriage of All Philosophical Trials in Theodicy' from 1791, which already includes both elements I am about to define.
4. Levinas, 'Useless Suffering,' 98.
5. Schelling, *Philosophical Investigations into the Essence of Human Freedom.*
6. See Forti, *New Demons.*

BIBLIOGRAPHY

Deleuze, Gilles and Guattari, Félix, *What is Philosophy?* trans. Hugh Tomlinson and Graham Burchell (New York: Columbia University Press, 1994).

Forti, Simona, *New Demons: Rethinking Power and Evil Today*, trans. Zakiya Hanafi (Stanford: Stanford University Press, 2014).

Kant, Immanuel, 'On the Miscarriage of All Philosophical Trials in Theodicy', in *Religion and Rational Theology*, eds. Allen Wood and George di Giovanni, trans. George di Giovanni (Cambridge: Cambridge University Press, 1996), 207–241.

Levinas, Emmanuel, 'Useless Suffering', in *Entre Nous: On Thinking-of-the-Other*, trans. Michael B. Smith and Barbara Harshav (New York: Columbia University Press, 1998).

Madeley, Richard, 'There are Devils Walking among Us', *The Daily Express*, May 16, 2020.

Schelling, F. W. J., *Philosophical Investigations into the Essence of Human Freedom*, trans. Jeff Love and Johannes Schmidt (Albany: SUNY Press, 2006).

18

DON'T,

Or the Thought Cat'apostrophed

Angel Delrez

What would a future [un avenir] be if the decision were able to be programmed, and if the risk [l'aléa], the uncertainty, the unstable certainty, the inassurance of the 'perhaps', were not suspended on it at the opening of what comes, flush with the event, within it and with an open heart?

– Jacques Derrida, in
The Politics of Friendship (1994)

The alternative to which is condemned today the thought could appear (to us) inevitable: *either* to endorse the polemic, that is to say to engage in an entrenched warfare (from the Greek πολεμικός, the polemic, that means 'that concerns war', or even 'war-specific'), *or* to reflect the after, *about* the after, that is to say about what should happen when we will get out – provided that we can get out – from a sanitary catastrophe whose end does not seem to stop to be postponed.

As doubly condemned to miss what, by dislocating time, seems no less than cracking the historical chain (past–present–future), the thought would thus no longer seem to have as its only alternative but to take part either in the prophylactic recapitulation of the ravages of bourgeois ideology, or in the strategic anticipation of what thought should strive to make happen. Thus turned either towards the past or towards the future, the thought would then be as if it were destined to turn away from the catastrophe, and this, at the risk of being able to approach it (at best) only from its before or its after: as it would exhaust itself in settling the catastrophe on what will have, if not announced, at least anticipated it or, conversely, on what will/would have to come to remedy it, the thought would no longer have as its sole and unique perspective that of bordering the event, that is to say of operating both below and beyond its arising.

But are these the only places of thought? Are these only the places of thought? Are they not rather the 'non-places' of thought, the 'places' in which thought, excepting itself from the catastrophe, is distracted from its originary responsibility?

This responsibility is the one which, recalling it to its etymology, enjoins the thought not less than to be the guarantor, not so much of the world, but of its suspension, of the suspension of the world. *Tenant du* (holding from) suspense, but also and above all *tenant au* (holding to) suspense (from the Latin verb pendere, 'penser' ('to think'), is 'to be suspended'), it appears in fact that it is more than ever imperative for thought, in and by the favour of thought, to pay attention not to give up too hastily to what, so to speak, constitutes it 'properly', namely its 'power(lessness)' of ex-position – to the time of the impossible.

Thus Giorgio Agamben points out in *La fine del pensiero*:

> In the Italian language, the word 'pensiero' (thought) originally had the meaning of anguish, of anxiety, which it still has, in the familiar expression: 'stare in pensiero'. The Latin verb pendere, from which the word derives from the Romance languages, it means 'stare in sospeso' (hanging in the suspension).[1]

Assuredly, there would be no question here of contesting the legitimacy of the 'reflections' which, seeking to resolve it, intend to conjugate the catastrophe at the past or even at the past future. Who could still decently disengage himself from the actions to file a lawsuit, in France and elsewhere, against the 'assholes who govern us'?[2] Who, except for some shameless fool, as impudent as he is imprudent, could still maintain, as Jean-Louis Bouchez, a Belgian senator and president of the *Mouvement Réformateur* (*MR*), claimed, that we are today only dealing with 'a fatality that says nothing about our system'?[3] Who could still deny that, faced to the pandemic, we were not all in the same boat, when (class reflex) the better-off rushed to exile themselves to the countryside or to buy private islands[4] – when they did not prefer, rather, to rush to take refuge in their 'air-filtering' bunkers[5] or to confine themselves, like King Maha Vajiralongkorn, aka Rama X, in luxury hotels, surrounded by their harems?[6] Who could even tolerate that, in an open letter to his employees, a billionaire exiled on his private island in the British Virgin Islands, Richard Branson, not to mention his name, the 312th world fortune, could claim, in order to save his airline (Virgin Atlantic), financial aid from a state to which, a few years earlier, he had recommended (healthy competition obliges) not to bail out British Airways and to let it go bankrupt?[7] Who, even supposing, as the aforementioned senator tweeted, that 'the Spanish flu and the great epidemics in the Middle Ages did not wait for globalization', could still deny that 'the exodus of the rich and the notable, the powerful and the wealthy is a constant in the long history of epidemics' and that if 'the rich do not die like the poor', it is above all 'because they do not live like them'?[8]

Yet, and for all that, we will argue that thought (provided that, by identifying its specificity, we can discern it from the soothing 'on reflection' and other 'after reflection') cannot be limited to these 'condemnations', which we know all too well, as Jean-Clet Martin pointed out, for being, 'in any case', 'always quickly established', they could not or, rather, should not be able to appease 'anyone', and 'especially not the philosopher' who, never, neither 'finds a position, nor finds a posture in the carrying out of a trial'.[9] This is why, if reflection, operating by withdrawing into oneself – 'reflection, as Maurice Blondel analyses in an observation addressed to the *Lalande*, implies [first of all] a redoubling [. . .], and as a withdrawal of psychological life into itself'[10] – denies the catastrophe, thought, for its part, ex-poses itself to it and inter-poses itself in it – to respond, within the interval, for its apostrophe or, we might say, with Jacques Derrida, for its 'cat'apostrophe'.

Of course, *from* reflection *to* thought, *between* reflection *and* thought, it might seem, as it is said in French, *n'y avoir qu'un pas* (literally: there is only a 'pas', a 'step' *and* a 'not', a 'step/not',[11] and figuratively: there is a small difference), *à peine un pas* (almost not a 'pas'). *Un pas – à peine.*[12] But to reflection, which skips and crosses it, this *pas*, the thought, on the contrary, intercedes for it. And marks it – *de ce pas* (literally: by this 'step/not', and figuratively: forthwith); with this suspended *pas*, so well-illustrated by the elided 'do not' of the English language: 'don't', in which would come to be translated the impossible '*don*' (gift) of an instant 't'. Is it necessary to recall it? The apostrophe, in articulatory phonetics, is also the typographic sign of a 'glottal stop', that is the symbol of an inter'ruption of the order of discourse.

Apostrophed by the catastrophe, cat'apostrophed therefore, thought as such cannot submit to the alternative to which those who own power, on all political sides, consider it preferable to force it, in a hurry *de la mettre au pas* (literally: put to the 'pas' and figuratively: bring to heel), if not to the blacklist. Unlike the (too) many 'reflections' that now obsess our screens and are all talk, thought doesn't breathe a word. It cannot economize the catastrophe. Therefore, to those who intimate it to express itself, the thought *ne dit rien qui vaille* (literally: 'says nothing worthwhile' and figuratively: 'it makes them suspicious'). *S'inter'disant* (telling itself in the inter'), it says 'no comment'.

'All the partisans of the great evenings and glorious awakenings, of the 'never again' and the 'day after', delude themselves with their great tirades. After the moment of truth of the catastrophe, new lies proliferate', Michaël Ferrier recently observed in the pages of *Le Monde*, before concluding: 'After, there is no after'.[13] Perhaps he didn't mean to say it so well. Because thinking the after, about the after, thinking about the future *and* at the future tense, wouldn't that be not only a lure, but a luxury, that of those wealthy people who, even before the announcements of deconfinement, were worried above all about planning their next holidays?

> Imagining the 'after world', unfortunately, with all due respect to the most honest people, remains a luxury, reminded us a collective coordinated by Mohamed Mechmache and Antoine Lagneau in a remarkable tribune. A luxury that cannot be afforded by those for whom the brutality of today's world is a reality from which it is impossible to escape. A luxury for those who can telework while others have to go to work every morning, sick with fear of contracting the virus. In working-class neighbourhoods, in order to dream of the after, the present should already be decent. Yet the daily routine is still one of indecency, social and ecological injustice and stigmatization. Coronavirus or not, the future is never really palpable here and the horizon is often precisely an impassable one [. . .]. The world of an enchanted tomorrow [. . .] cannot wait for a hypothetical after.

Therefore, it is no longer even possible to conjugate it, this 'hypothetical after', at the future, since there is nothing more to expect from it. From the future, there is nothing to expect. 'After, there is no after'. The catastrophe has already happened. *Toujours déjà*, it has taken us by surprise – whatever we could have said or could still say or find fault with. So, of what will come, perhaps, in the very mode of perhaps, of that perhaps which, as Derrida pointed out, 'there is no more just category for the future',[14] thought has nothing to say for the moment. For the moment, that goes without saying – the thought. *Et peut-être n'est-ce pas plus mal.*

NOTES

1. Agamben, 'La Fine del pensiero' my translation.
2. See Lordon, 'Les connards qui nous gouvernent'.
3. On 29 March 2020, Georges-Louis Bouchez tweeted: 'the Spanish flu and the great epidemics in the Middle Ages did not wait for globalization . . . I think we need to stop making great theories about the end of the world. This is a fatality that says nothing about our system' (my translation).
4. Sautreuil, 'Îles désertes, bunkers, jets privés'.
5. 'Coronavirus: Les millionnaires se ruent sur les bunkers de luxe', *CNWES*.
6. See Aujla Poonam Singh, 'Coronavirus: le roi de Thaïlande se confine dans un hôtel avec son harem' and Vincelot, 'Le roi de Thaïlande confiné avec 20 femmes captives'.
7. Delesalle-Stolper, 'Sur son île, le milliardaire Richard Branson confiné hors de la réalité'.
8. Benbassa and Attias, 'Déserter les villes pour les champs en cas d'épidémie' (my translation).
9. Martin, 'Vivre après?' (my translation).
10. Lalande, 'Sur Réflexion', 905 (my translation).
11. The French word 'pas' means both 'step' and 'not'. In this paragraph, we always use it keeping this double meaning.
12. On this issue, see Derrida, 'A peine', in *Mémoires: for Paul de Man*, xxiii:

> How would one translate *à peine*? If one translate *à peine* by the equivalent of *presque* or rather *presque pas* (scarcely, hardly, almost not) or by the equivalent of 'tout près de rien' (nearly not or nearly no) one would lose by the wayside the name or noun of *peine*, which virtually takes shelter, is hidden, almost disappearing, even for a French ear lulled a bit by that which we call 'ordinary language'. In the expression *à peine*, the French would hardly have heard the hard, the dash or the pain, the difficulty that there is or the trouble that one gives oneself. 'Hardly' might be the best approximation. The French ear hardly [*à peine*] perceives the sense of hardly [*à peine*].

13. Ferrier, 'La littérature prend le contre-pied des discours qui visent à atténuer une catastrophe', 28 (my translation).
14. Derrida, *The Politics of Friendship*, 29.

BIBLIOGRAPHY

Agamben, Giorgio. 'La Fine del pensiero', translated by G. Macé, *Le Nouveau Commerce*, 1982, 53–54.

Benbassa, Esther and Jean-Christophe Attias. 'Déserter les villes pour les champs en cas d'épidémie, un vieux réflexe de classe', *Libération*, 2 avril 2020. https://

www.liberation.fr/debats/2020/04/02/deserter-les-villes-pour-les-champs-en-cas-d-epidemie-un-vieux-reflexe-de-classe_1783934.

'Coronavirus: Les millionnaires se ruent sur les bunkers de luxe', *CNWES*, 27 mars 2020. https://www.cnews.fr/monde/2020-03-27/coronavirus-les-millionnaires-se-ruent-sur-les-bunkers-de-luxe-940853.

Delesalle-Stolper, Sonia. 'Sur son île, le milliardaire Richard Branson confiné hors de la réalité', *Libération*, 30 avril 2020. https://www.liberation.fr/planete/2020/04/30/sur-son-ile-le-milliardaire-richard-branson-confine-hors-de-la-realite_1786840.

Derrida, Jacques. 'A peine', in *Mémoires: for Paul de Man*. Translated by C. Lyndsay, J. Culler, E. Cadava and P. Kamuf. New York: Columbia University Press, 1989.

Derrida, Jacques. *The Politics of Friendship*. Translated by G. Collin. London: Verso, 2005.

Ferrier, Michaël. 'La littérature prend le contre-pied des discours qui visent à atténuer une catastrophe', *Le Monde*, Dimanche 24–Lundi 25 mai 2020. https://www.lemonde.fr/idees/article/2020/05/24/michael-ferrier-la-litterature-vient-prendre-le-contre-pied-des-discours-qui-visent-a-attenuer-une-catastrophe_6040565_3232.html.

Lalande, André. 'Sur Réflexion', in *Vocabulaire technique et critique de la philosophie* (Volume 2: N-Z). Paris: PUF, 1997.

Lordon, Frédéric, 'Les connards qui nous gouvernent', *La pompe à phynance*, 19 mars 2020. https://blog.mondediplo.net/les-connards-qui-nous-gouvernent.

Martin, Jean-Clet. 'Vivre après?', *Philosopher en temps d'épidémie* (n°9), 23 mars 2020. https://www.youtube.com/watch?v=lr_HCVjxfo4.

Poonam Singh, Aujla. 'Coronavirus: le roi de Thaïlande se confine dans un hôtel avec son harem', *The Huffington post*, 30 mars 2020. https://www.huffingtonpost.fr/entry/le-roi-de-thailande-confine-dans-un-grand-hotel-allemand-son-harem-de-20-femmes_fr_5e81914cc5b6cb9dc1a2fb83.

Sautreuil, Pierre. 'Îles désertes, bunkers, jets privés: comment les super riches réagissent-ils face au coronavirus?', *Le Figaro*, 25 mars 2020. https://www.lefigaro.fr/iles-desertes-bunkers-jets-prives-comment-les-super-riches-reagissent-face-au-coronavirus-nbsp-20200325.

Vincelot, Sophie. 'Le roi de Thaïlande confiné avec 20 femmes captives: de nouvelles révélations sordides', *Gala*, 3 avril 2020. https://www.gala.fr/l_actu/news_de_stars/le-roi-de-thailande-confine-avec-20-femmes-captives-de-nouvelles-revelations-sordides_446086.

INDEX

ABOUT THE CONTRIBUTORS AND TRANSLATORS

Aïdas Sanogo is a social anthropologist who specializes in urban land governance. She lectures at the Centre Universitaire de Manga, Burkina Faso. Her current research compares land tenure systems in urban West Africa, with a specific focus on three secondary cities: Kumasi in Ghana, Bouaké in Côte d'Ivoire and Bobo Dioulasso in Burkina Faso. Rooted in the field of urban and political anthropology, drawing on multisited ethnographic fieldwork, this research project looks into the intertwined links between urban dwellers' discourses and practices related to land tenure. Using a diversity of land conflicts as an entry point, she analyses how heterogeneous groups of social actors involved in urban land governance constantly (re) shape their understanding of urbanity.

Angel Delrez is an international PhD student at Université Paris Nanterre (Sophiapol laboratory) and Università degli studi di Torino (consortium FINO). His doctoral thesis titled 'Marx, Derrida ant the time of the capital', concerns the issues of what he calls the 'heritage of-Derrida-of-Marx'. In his recent publications and/or talks, we find 'Un spectre hante l'Europe: le spectre de la clandestinité' (2018); 'Avec Derrida, répondre de Marx' (2019); '"Everything burns", ou la société de consumation' (2019); and 'Dell'eredità di-Derrida-di-Marx' (2020).

Benedetta Todaro is a psychologist and psychoanalyst based in Paris. She is currently a PhD student in Philosophy at the Université Paris-Est Créteil and a Temporary Teacher and Researcher at the Université de Picardie Jules Verne. Her current research, at the crossroads of psychology and philosophy, focuses on the question of the body in Western society.

Daniel J. Smith is assistant professor of philosophy at University of Memphis. He received his PhD from Penn State in 2018 and has published numerous articles on a variety of figures including Deleuze, Foucault, Derrida and Hegel. He is currently writing a book on the concept of 'evil' in German Idealism.

Divya Dwivedi is a philosopher based in the Subcontinent. She is associate professor of philosophy and literature in the Department of Humanities and Social Sciences, Indian Institute of Technology, Delhi. She is the co-author with Shaj Mohan of *Gandhi and Philosophy*: *On Theological Anti-Politics*. She coedited *Narratology and Ideology* (2018) and *Public Sphere from outside the West* (2015). She has recently edited 'L'Inde: Colossale et Capitale', a special issue of the revue Critique (Éditions Minuit 872–873, January 2020), a special issue of *Revue des femmes philosophes* no. 4–5 (titled Intellectuels, Philosophes, Femmes en Inde: des espèces en danger, CNRS-UNESCO, 2017).

Federico Ferrari teaches Philosophy of Art at Brera Academy of Fine Arts in Milan. He was correspondent for the Collège International de Philosophie. Among his publications are *La comunità errante. Bataille e l'esperienza comunitaria* (1997), *Nudità. Per una critica silenziosa* (1999), *L'insieme vuoto. Per una pragmatica dell'immagine* (2013), *L'anarca* (2014), *Oscillazioni* (2016) and with Jean-Luc Nancy her has published *Nus sommes* (2002), *Iconographie de l'auteur* (2005) and *La fin des fins* (2015). He is the founder, with Andrea Cortellessa and Riccardo Venturi, of www.antinomie.it

Ivana Perica is the author of *Die privat-öffentliche Achse des Politischen: Das Unvernehmen zwi-schen Hannah Arendt und Jacques Rancière* (2016). After the completion of her PhD at the University of Vienna, she taught in the Department of Political Science at the University of Vienna and the University of Applied Arts Vienna. Since March 2019, she has been a Postdoctoral Researcher at LMU Munich (DFG Research Training Group 'Globalization and Literature: Representations, Transformations, Interventions'), where she is pursuing a habilitation project on political literature around the fracture points of 1928 and 1968.

Jan Völker is a research associate at the Institute of Fine Arts and Aesthetics at the Berlin University of the Arts, associate professor at the Institute of Philosophy of the Slovenian Academy of Arts and Sciences in Ljubljana and teaches at Bard College Berlin. His current work focuses on the division of modern thought between Marx, Freud, Kant and Hegel. Recent Publications include (as editor and translator) 'German Philosophy', a debate between Alain Badiou and Jean-Luc Nancy (MIT, 2018); *Badiou and the German Tradition of Philosophy* (edited, 2019).

Jean-Luc Nancy is Distinguished Professor of Philosophy at the University of Strasbourg and one of France's foremost intellectuals. His work spans over dozens of books, hundreds of articles, addressing a diverse set of topics, including community, religion and the body as well as the major figures of the modern intellectual tradition. Some of his major works include: *La communauté désœuvrée* (1986), *L'expérience de la liberté* (1988), *Une pensée finie* (1990), *Corpus* (1992), *Être singulier pluriel* (1996), *L' « il y a » du rapport sexuel* (2001), *Déconstruction du christianisme* (2005–10), *L'intrus* (2010), *La possibilité d'un monde* (2013), *La communauté désavouée* (2014) and *Que faire ?* (2016).

Juan Manuel Garrido teaches philosophy at Alberto Hurtado University, Santiago de Chile. His research interests include the philosophical concept of life and the philosophy of knowledge production and scientific practice. Among his publications are *La formation des formes* (2008), *On Time, Being and Hunger: Challenging the Traditional Way of Thinking Life* (2012) and *Producción de conocimiento* (2018).

Marcia Sá Cavalcante Schuback is professor of philosophy at Södertörn University in Sweden. She studied philosophy at Albert-Ludwigs Universitet in Freiburg in Breisgau, Germany, under the supervision of Prof. Ute Guzzoni. Back in Brazil, Schuback translated Heidegger's Being and Time (1989) into Portuguese. Between 1985 and 1992, she worked as coordinator for the cultural section of the Forum for Science and Culture of the University Federal of Rio de Janeiro where she was the editor of the magazine on Philosophy and Aesthetics *Arte e Palavra*. Her recent books are *Time in Exile: In Conversation with Heidegger, Blanchot, and Lispector* (2020) and *O fascismo da ambiguidade: um ensaio conceitual* (2021).

M. Lucía Rivera S. received her PhD from the Universidad Nacional de Colombia. She was postdoctoral researcher in Bioethics with Universidad El Bosque and she is now associate professor of Bioethics at Universidad El Bosque, Bogotá Colombia. She is the founding member of the Red Colombiana de Mujeres Filósofas, member of the Consultive Commitee of the Red de Mujeres Filósofas de América Latina UNESCO and member of Redbioética UNESCO.

Osamu Nishitani is a philosopher and professor emeritus of Tokyo University of Foreign Studies. Born in 1950, he is the author of 'Wonderland' of Immortality, Critical Phase of the Universal History, What Is the War on Terror? America, System of Liberty, etc.

Parham Shahrjerdi was born in 1980 in Teheran and is now based in Paris. Writer, critic, editor and translator, he is the founder of the website Espace Maurice Blanchot (blanchot.fr) and the co-founder of the magazine *Hors-Sol* (hors-sol.net). Publisher of important works of the new Iranian literature (banned by censorship) and, in Persian, of works by J. Baudrillard, J. Butler, G. Deleuze and G. Fighting.

Pierre Nakoulima is professor at the University Joseph Ki Zerbo of Ouagadougou and president of the Manga University Center. He has numerous publications on development and environmental issues. He heads the 'Crisis, Mutations and Conflict Management' Laboratory.

S. Romi Mukherjee is professor of social sciences at New York University in Paris and visiting lecturer in the political humanities at *L'Institut d'études politiques de Paris* (Sciences Po). He has published widely, mostly in political theory, philosophy and the history of religions. Recent monographs and edited volumes include: *Durkheim and Violence* (2010), *Social Memory and Hypermodernity* (2012, with Éric Brian and Marie Jaisson), *The Political Anthropology of the Global* (2013), *Nouveaux visages du religieux dans un monde sécularisé* (2014, with Lionel Obadia) and *Inequality in the Age of Neo-Liberalism* (2018, with Beth Epstein, Janie Pellaby and Réjane Senac).

Sergio Benvenuto is a psychoanalyst and philosopher living in Rome. He is researcher at the National Council for Scientific Research (CNR) in Rome, Italy. He is the president of Institute for Advanced Studies in psychoanalysis (ISAP) in Italy. Since 1995 until 2020 he is the editor of *EJP. European Journal of Psychoanalysis* and is a member of the Editorial Board of *American Imago* and *Psychoanalytic Discourse*.

He has worked on Freud and Lacan, Wittgenstein and ethics, Plato's philosophy of Eros, Theory of Fashion, Theory of populism and Monotheisms (with J.-L. Nancy). His publications, in many different languages, include: with A. Molino, *In Freud's Tracks* (2008); 'Ethics, Wonder and Real in Wittgenstein', in Y. Gustafsson, C. Kronqvist, H. Nykänen, eds., *Ethics and the Philosophy of Culture: Wittgensteinian Approaches* (2013); *What Are Perversions?* (2016); *Conversations with Lacan* (2020); three chapters in *Coronavirus, Psychoanalysis, and Philosophy Conversations on Pandemics, Politics and Society*.

Tadeusz Koczanowicz holds a BA and MA in Sociology and a MA in Cultural Studies from the University of Warsaw. He is currently completing a PhD in Slavic literature at the University of Zürich, where he is part of the *Crisis and Communitas* project sponsored by the SNSF. In his doctoral project he explores alternatives to nation-state-based politics in Polish culture. Apart from academic work he also writes political analysis.

ABOUT THE TRANSLATORS

Chloé Pretesacque is a PhD candidate, at La Sorbonne, and a translator. She works through various fields in the humanities. Using different tools ranging from aesthetics, philosophy of sciences, gender studies or enlarged anthropology, she holds a deep interest for the contemporary metaphorical figures of mushrooms and jellyfishes. Following them as guides into stories from the subterrestrial and submarine world, she proposes alternative narrations for alternative futures.

Sindhuja Veeraragavan is a literary translator based in India, working predominantly between French and English languages. Her translations include *Electric Nights in Beijing* by Nicolas Idier and *Smart* by Frederic Martel. She holds an MPhil in French from Jawaharlal Nehru University.

www.ingramcontent.com/pod-product-compliance
Ingram Content Group UK Ltd.
Pitfield, Milton Keynes, MK11 3LW, UK
UKHW041636031026
15587UKWH00001B/323

9 781538 164709